THEN & NOW®

GRAVESEND, BROOKLYN

Opposite: In this watercolor of the rear of No. 15–17 Gravesend Neck Road, artist Charles W. Bauhan (1861–1938) captured Homer Wiltse (about 1820–1898) tending his garden in 1893, the year before Brooklyn annexed Gravesend. (Author's collection.)

THEN & NOW®

GRAVESEND, BROOKLYN

Joseph Ditta

For my father, Joseph P. Ditta (1928–2002), who always found time to follow me "here and there" around Gravesend. Thanks for coming.

ISBN 978-0-7385-6469-2

Library of Congress Control Number: 2008939826

Published by Arcadia Publishing
Charleston, South Carolina

Printed in the United States of America

For all general information contact Arcadia Publishing at:
Telephone 843-853-2070
Fax 843-853-0044
E-mail sales@arcadiapublishing.com
For customer service and orders:
Toll-Free 1-888-313-2665

Visit us on the Internet at www.arcadiapublishing.com

On the front cover: Just three families have occupied Gravesend's idyllic Wyckoff-Bennett-Mont house (shown in 1924 and today): the Wyckoffs, who built it before 1766; the Bennetts, who bought it in 1835; and the Monts, who have owned it since 1983. See page 61 for further details. (Author's collection.)

On the back cover: On Christmas Day 1897, the barber Francesco Micucci hosted the first mass of the Roman Catholic parish of SS. Simon and Jude in his shop at 321 Avenue T, the building left of center in this 1915 view up Gravesend (now McDonald) Avenue. See page 71 for more on the church and page 72 for a contemporary photograph of this spot. (Author's collection.)

Contents

Acknowledgments

This book would be substantially incomplete without the 10 historic views included courtesy of John Antonides, Albert C. Simmel Jr., Michael V. Susi, the Varacalli family, and the New-York Historical Society. Excepting these, all archival images are from the author's collection. All contemporary photographs were taken by the author.

The opportunity to visit their historic properties was graciously provided by Dr. Justin L. Anderson, John Antonides, Annette and Stuart Mont, Armond Sorrentino, and Dennis Ferrara of the Varuna Boat Club. Ceil Kaufman welcomed me into her backyard to photograph the most awesome sight in Sea Gate.

Erin L. Vosgien, junior publisher at Arcadia, saw a need for this book the moment I proposed it. She made each step of the project enjoyable.

Inspiration came largely from the example of my good friend Michael V. Susi, whose own Arcadia Publishing titles are models of precision.

All my colleagues at the library of the New-York Historical Society helped in some way, but for their guidance I am especially grateful to Jean W. Ashton and Nina Nazionale. In the Department of Rights and Reproductions, Eleanor Gillers and Glenn Castellano supplied my requested images with their usual seamless efficiency.

Friends and relatives who shared information and offered encouragement include John Antonides, Lon Black, Liz Call, Barbara Capeci, Louis Castaldo, Theresa Cyran, Kristy DiCario, Gale Harris, Eric J. Ierardi (founder and president of the Gravesend Historical Society, without whose efforts what little survives from Gravesend's past would be lost), Patrice Ingrassia, Frank Kools, Lionel R. Lindsay (author of the 2004 memoir *Gravesend Kid: A Brooklyn Boyhood*), Alyssa Loorya and Christopher Ricciardi, Janet and Dominick Marrano, Brian Merlis, Marie M. Moore (who keeps Gravesend alive in Santa Fe), Francis Morrone, Richard Rahn, Sean Sawyer (a walking encyclopedia of architectural styles), Catherine and Donald Sbordone, Ken Siegelman, Marietta Starace Stapleton, Bob Stonehill, Rich Stremme, Diana Stuart and Ira Kluger, Jay and Nick Varacalli, and the generous Van Sicklen family descendants Martha J. Waldner, Albert C. Simmel Jr., Justina Simmel, Timothy S. Barry, and the late Charles Van Sicklen Mottola and his widow, the lovely Virginia.

Last, but never least, for their love, support, chauffeuring skills, and valiant attempts not to roll their eyes every time I said "Gravesend," I thank my mother, Annette; my sister, Denise; my brother-in-law, Joseph Scannapieco; and my partner, Michael D. Riley, whose expert reading kept "the refuse of encroaching urbanization" off these pages.

Introduction

Ultima Thule was a region the ancients believed lay at the end of the Earth. In Roz Chast's *New Yorker* cartoon with that title (published on October 14, 2002), a mother warns her daughter of the dangers lurking in the neighborhoods of Brooklyn, New York, outside their own. Heedless, the girl sets out to explore and steps off the planet. "I just wanted to see what was on the other side of McDonald Avenue!" she wails.

What Chast's character probably did not know is that McDonald Avenue was once called Gravesend Avenue (see page 72). If she had followed it south to a point just below Avenue U, she would have come to the heart of Gravesend, one of the first planned communities in America. She would not have recognized it as such. There are no historic signs to read, just the names on auto body shops under the elevated train tracks. It might seem like the gritty edge of the world today, but to its founder, Lady Moody, Gravesend was Utopia.

Deborah Moody (born about 1586 and died about 1659) was the wealthy, freethinking widow of a baronet who left England when the Court of the Star Chamber ordered that she limit her time in London and stay on her Wiltshire estate. By 1639, she was in Puritan Massachusetts, where her dissenting belief that scripture did not sanction infant baptism branded her "a dangerous woman." Avoiding censure she moved in 1643 to New Netherland, where she petitioned the tolerant Dutch to grant her and some followers a spot on which to worship as they pleased.

A war raging against the Native Americans foiled the group's immediate plans. After the hostilities, on December 19, 1645, Director-General Willem Kieft issued a patent for land on southwestern Long Island, an area that by mid-century included five Dutch towns: Flatbush, Flatlands, New Utrecht, Bushwick, and Brooklyn. Kieft's patent called this sixth, English town "Gravesand," a combination of two similar sounding European places: 's-Gravenzande, South Holland (which means "count's beach" in Dutch), and Gravesend, England (which takes its name from words meaning "at the end of the grove"). Eventually spelled the English way, Gravesend's seemingly morbid name had no connection to burials (despite the presence of New York City's earliest cemetery within its borders; see page 12).

Lady Moody's fellow patentee, the surveyor James Hubbard, designed the town's central plan: a 16-acre square bounded by present-day Village Road North, Village Road East, Village Road South, and Van Sicklen Street and cut into quadrants by the intersection of Gravesend Neck Road and McDonald Avenue (see the map on page 11). In each quadrant, 10 house lots bordered a common yard for holding livestock. A palisade enclosed the larger square and beyond it circled 40 long, wedge-shaped plantations. The pattern resembled a radiant cross and perhaps signified Lady Moody's intent—that Gravesend "shine" like a beacon for seekers of religious freedom. Kieft's patent ensured they could enjoy "liberty of Conscience . . . without molestation or disturbance from any magistrate or . . . ecclesiastical minister that may pretend jurisdiction over them."

This idealism died with Lady Moody. Soon many Gravesenders moved on to other ventures. Families that stayed (with surnames like Stillwell and Lake) were joined by their Dutch neighbors (with surnames like Stryker and Voorhies) whose language, church, and customs prevailed as intermarriage blurred ethnic distinctions. That English Gravesend became increasingly Dutch is clear from the numerous Dutch-style farmhouses in this book. (Only those on pages 21, 31, 59, 61, and 73 survive. Their projecting eaves are characteristic of the form.)

The British seized New Netherland in 1664 and renamed it New York. In 1683, they formed Kings County from the six towns on southwestern Long Island, but the six remained self-governing far into the 19th century. The town of Brooklyn incorporated as a city in 1834. Between 1854 and 1896, Brooklyn annexed each of its neighbors until its borders equaled Kings County's. Gravesend became the 31st ward of the City of Brooklyn on May 3, 1894. Brooklyn, in turn, became a borough of New York City on January 1, 1898.

Gravesend was roughly triangular, its apex pointed north to Foster Avenue and East Seventeenth Street, its eastern side along Gerritsen's Creek, its western side along Bay Parkway, and its base on the Atlantic Ocean. It covered much of the once marshy reaches of southern Brooklyn, including all or parts of the present neighborhoods of Homecrest, Sheepshead Bay, Plum(b) Beach, Gerritsen Beach, Marine Park, Madison, Midwood, Bensonhurst, Ulmer Park, and Manhattan Beach, Brighton Beach, and Sea Gate on Coney Island.

Coney Island proved key to the urbanization of Gravesend, which had a total population of 898 in 1845. Between 1862 and 1879, five steam railroads opened through town to carry well-off New Yorkers on trips to the shore, where luxury hotels and nearby racetracks sprang up to house and amuse them (see pages 63 and 74). Later electrified and linked to downtown Brooklyn and Manhattan, the trains next shuttled thousands of working-class immigrants to the area seeking spacious, modern homes (like those on pages 80–82) outside the city's aging tenements.

They found (and often built) their houses on a grid of numbered streets and alphabetical avenues mapped in 1874 in anticipation of Brooklyn's absorption of Gravesend. Many streets existed only on paper until the 20th century. When opened, some old structures blocking their paths were shifted to new property lines (see page 14), but as this book illustrates, demolition ruled the day. Gravesend's current landscape of asphalt and brick was largely complete by 1929, and in the intervening decades, most traces of its rural history have disappeared.

With a couple of exceptions, the old images in *Gravesend, Brooklyn* span the years 1879 to 1949, with a focus on 1900 to 1930, the period of Gravesend's greatest development. They come from postcards, photographs, prints, lantern slides, stereoscopic views, and one map and are divided geographically into three chapters.

While this book is meant as a guide to the changing sights of Gravesend, it is not an invitation to trespass. Please respect private property by keeping to the sidewalk or street when contemplating present and past.

CHAPTER 1

CENTRAL GRAVESEND

THE VILLAGE SQUARE

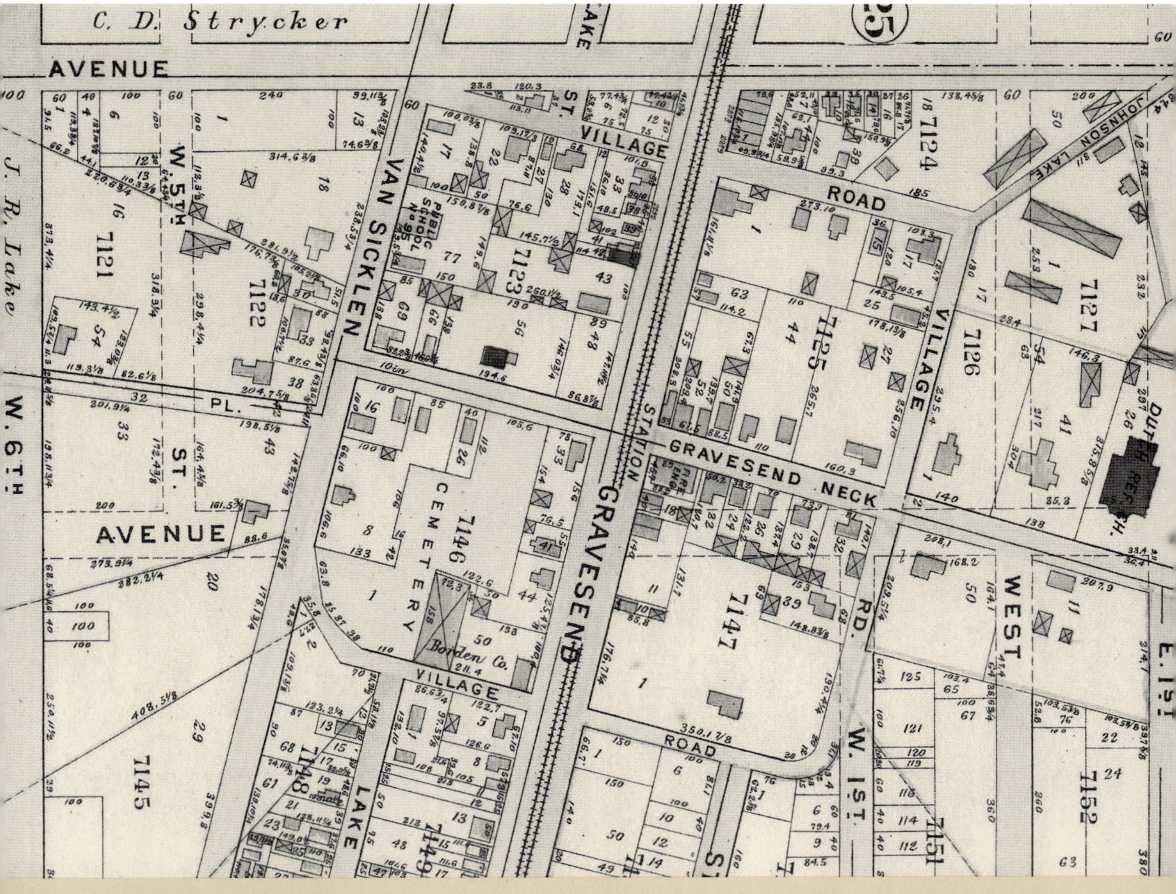

This 1907 map shows Gravesend's central village square 260 years after it was planned. Gravesend (now McDonald) Avenue cuts north–south across the middle, Gravesend Neck Road runs east–west, and Village Roads North, East, South, and Van Sicklen Street mark the perimeter. At left, traces of the town's original wedge-shaped plantations extend over a newer grid of numbered streets.

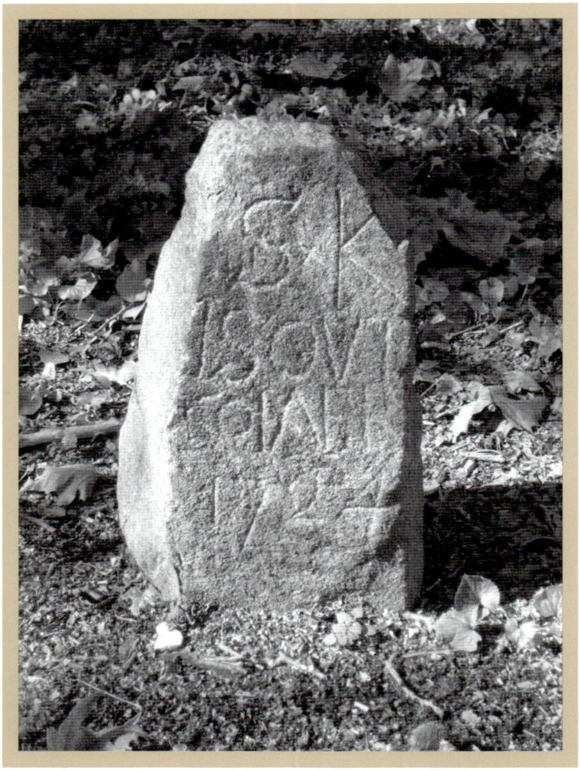

The Gravesend Cemetery is a tangible reminder of the area's early settlers. Established about 1650 in the southwestern quadrant of the town square, it grew to 1.6 acres by the 20th century. Its oldest surviving marker is a crudely carved fieldstone dated 1724. The Gravesend Historical Society secured landmark designation for the cemetery in 1976 and dedicated its present fence in 2002. The Van Sicklen family's private plot next to the Gravesend Neck Road gate received burials between 1842 and 1992.

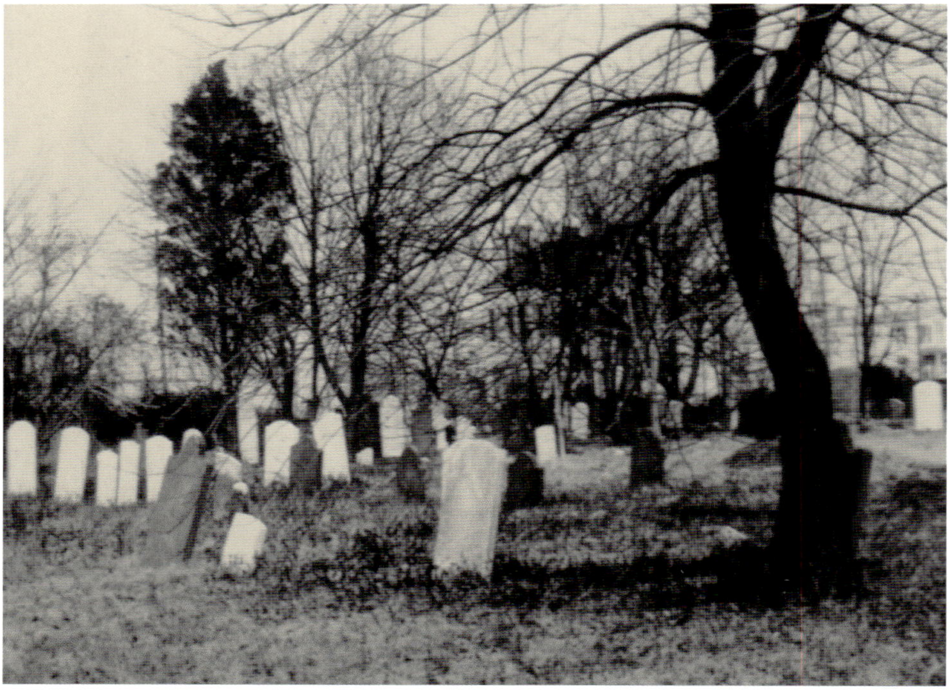

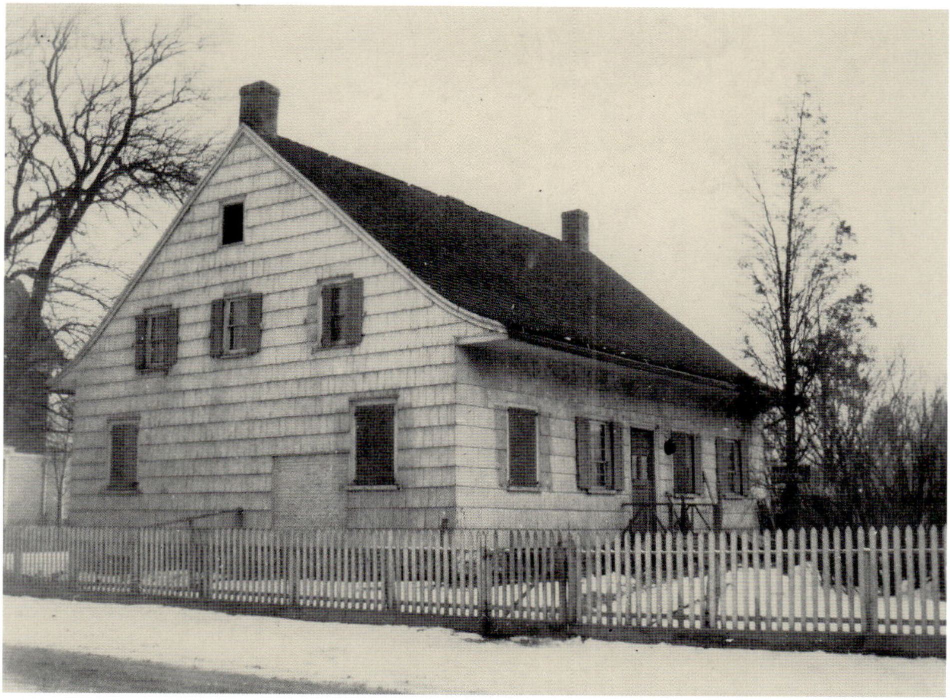

Englishman John Lake, progenitor of the Lake family, arrived in Gravesend by 1656. Around 1800, his great-grandson Daniel (1730–1810) built a farmhouse in the prevailing Dutch style at what became 377 Van Sicklen Street, seen here in 1923. It replaced an earlier Lake house and stood almost inside the Gravesend Cemetery. It was demolished about 1930 to build Corso Court, a cul-de-sac of 14 brick houses identified by a rare enamel street sign attached to No. 2.

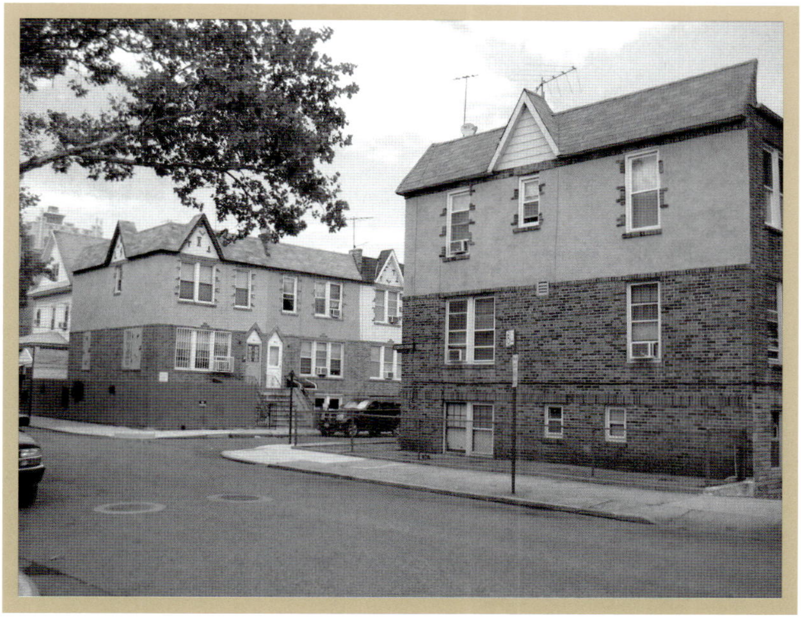

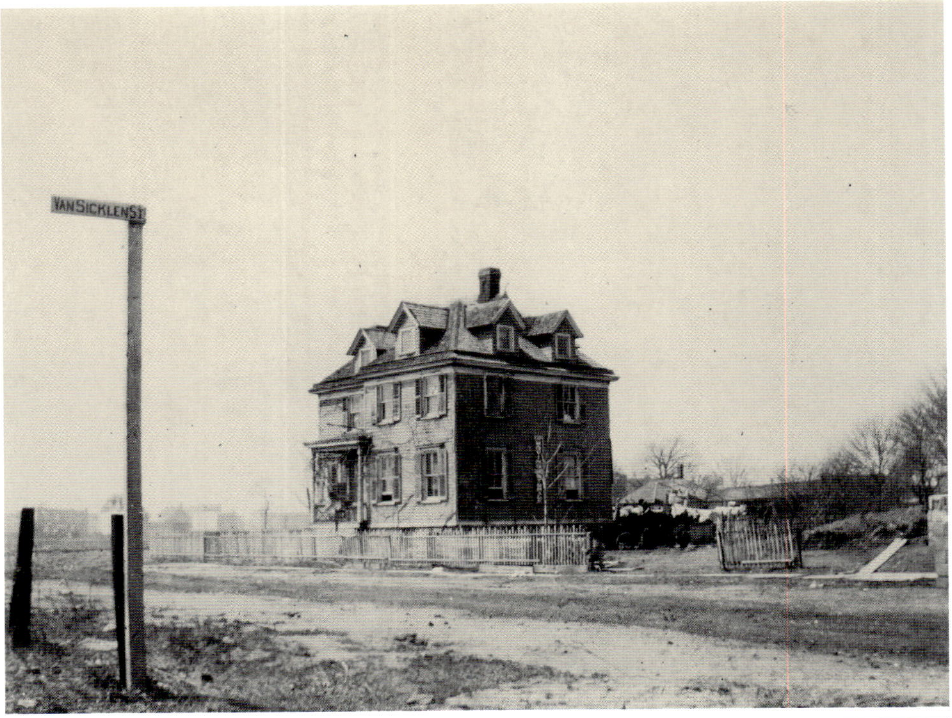

The Lake family owned at least five houses on the western edge of Gravesend's village square. Their surrounding farmland was known as Lake Place, a name now applied to the road that once bisected the property. Their late-19th-century home at 221 Avenue V, shown here in 1923, stood originally in the roadbed near Van Sicklen Street but was shifted to this address between 1912 and 1920. It was demolished in 2003 to build two brick condominiums.

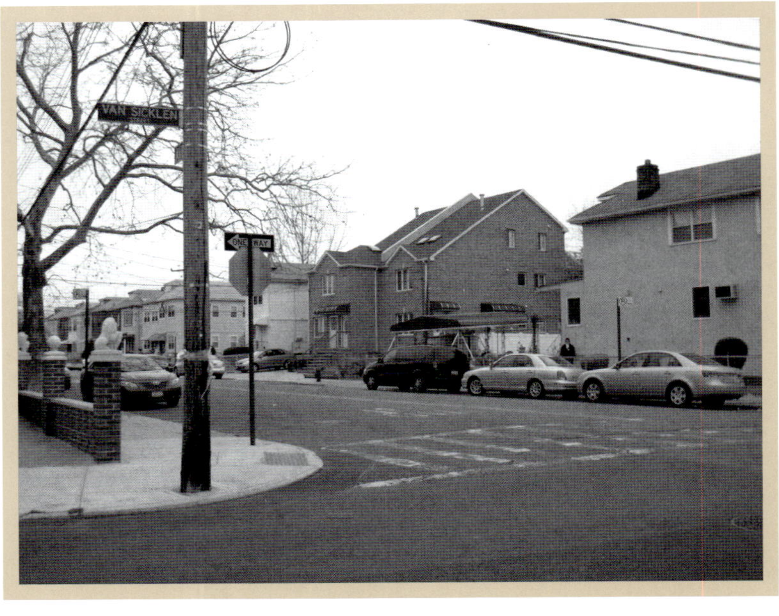

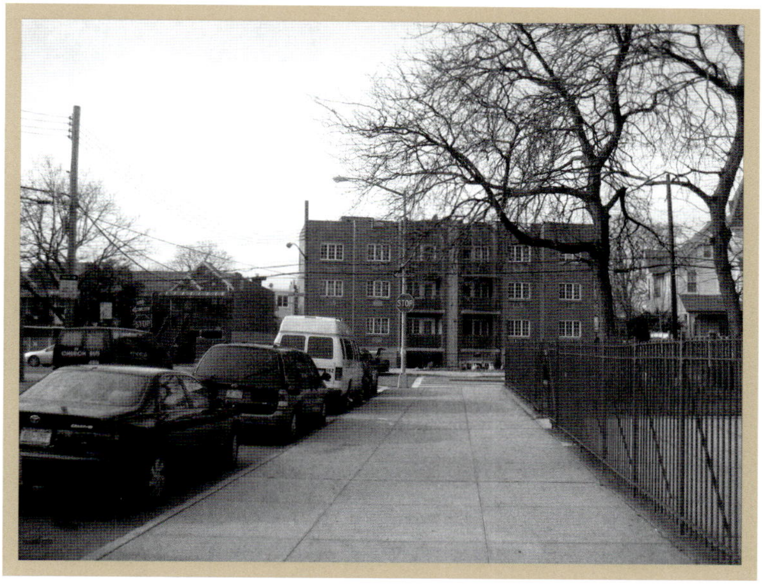

No. 2 Lake Place, the 1880s house at left in the 1923 photograph, belonged to building contractor William B. Lake (1852–1934), who died tragically after being struck by a car while walking to the Gravesend Reformed Dutch Church. The house at right, 354 Van Sicklen Street, was an earlier Lake residence. It probably dated from the 1830s and stood—clad in pink aluminum siding—until 1989. Its high fieldstone wall was destroyed early in 2008.

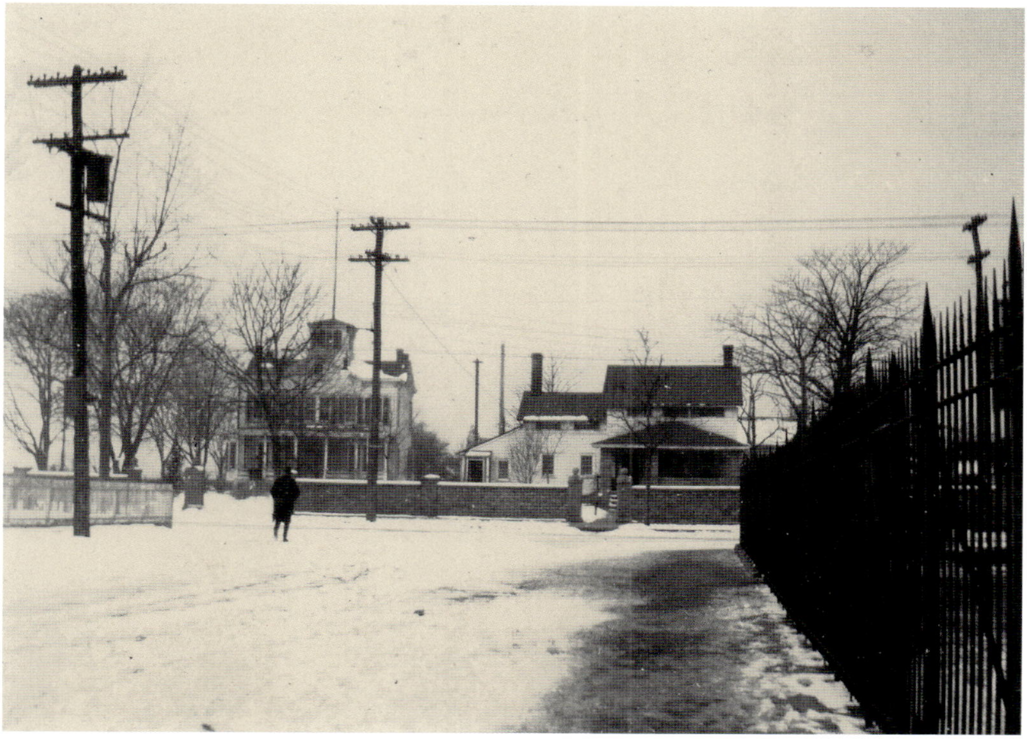

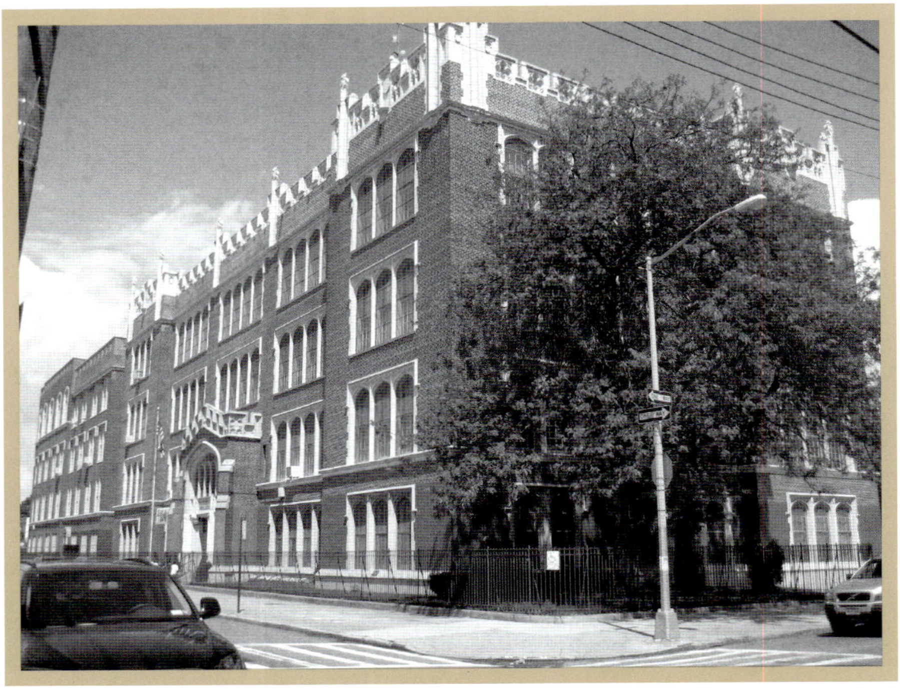

The turreted cottage at right in the *c.* 1913 view was originally home to Judge Anthony Waring. It stood diagonally north across Van Sicklen Street from the similar Stryker house (No. 346), and later served as an annex to the adjacent schoolhouse of P.S. 95. Among the first buildings affected by construction of the current brick school (its older portion dates from 1915), the Waring house was moved around 1914 to 2064 West Sixth Street.

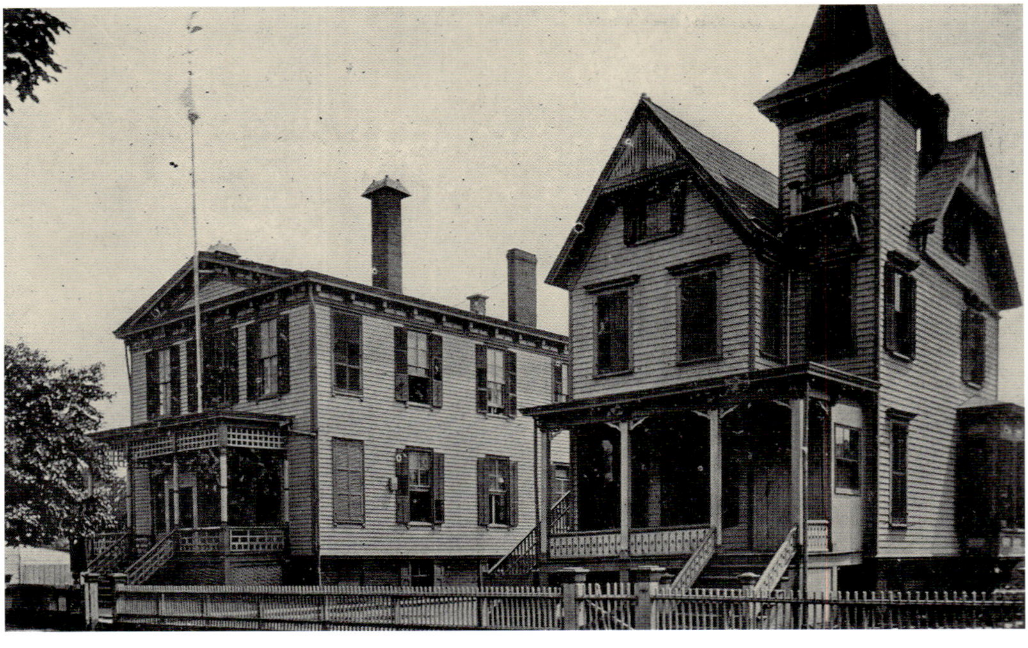

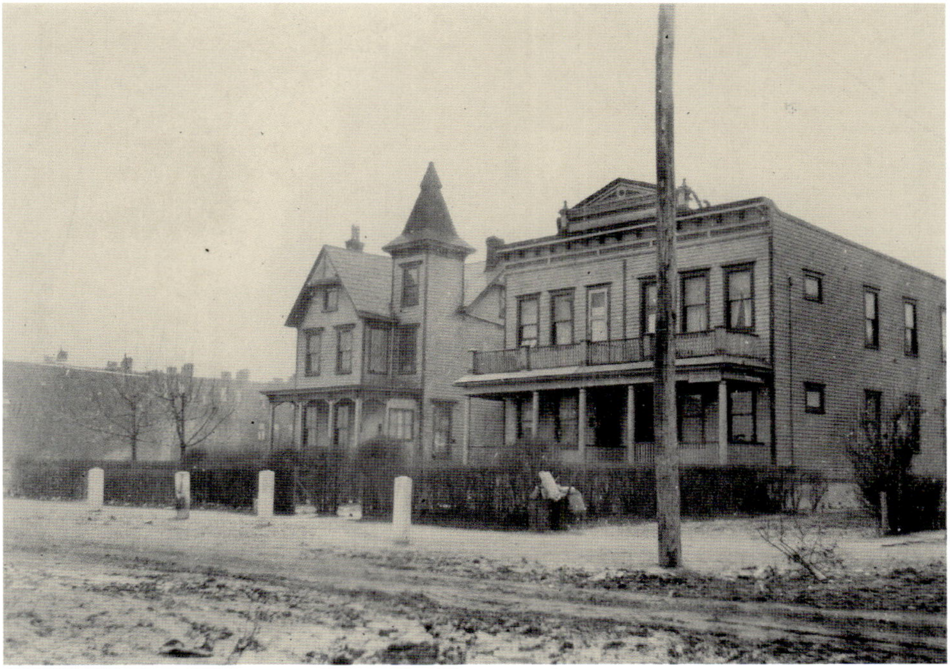

Around 1914, the annex of P.S. 95, formerly Judge Anthony Waring's house, was moved off its original site on the east side of Van Sicklen Street to make way for the 1915 portion of the present school. It has stood since then at 2064 West Sixth Street (at left in both photographs), where recent cosmetic changes fail to mask its distinctive shape. The four stone slabs lining the curb in the 1923 view are horse hitching posts.

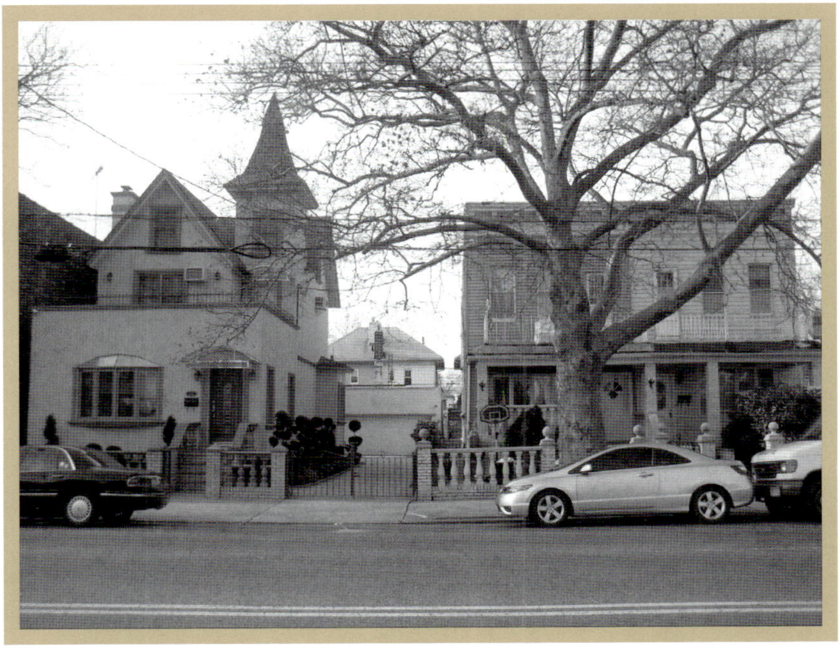

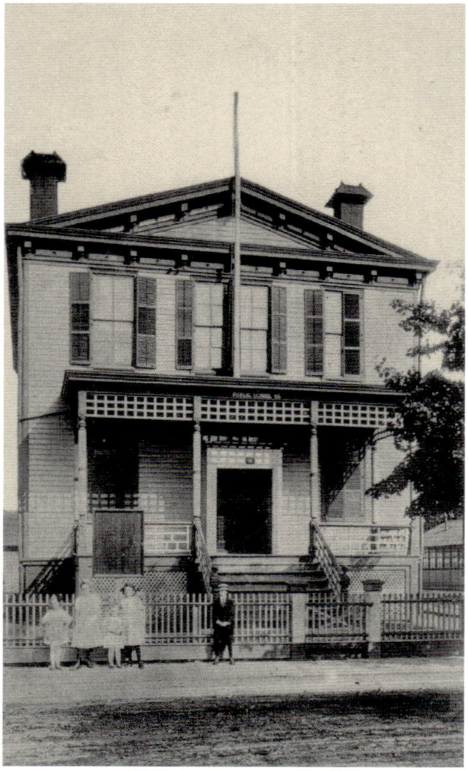

Gravesend's first school opened in 1728 on a site later taken by the town hall on McDonald Avenue. Since 1838, its District No. 1 school—renamed P.S. 95 when Brooklyn annexed Gravesend—has occupied the east side of Van Sicklen Street, north of Gravesend Neck Road. The 1888 schoolhouse in the *c.* 1910 image stood opposite Lama Court. It survived beside the 1915 brick structure (No. 345 Van Sicklen Street) until a 1939 addition to that building forced its demolition.

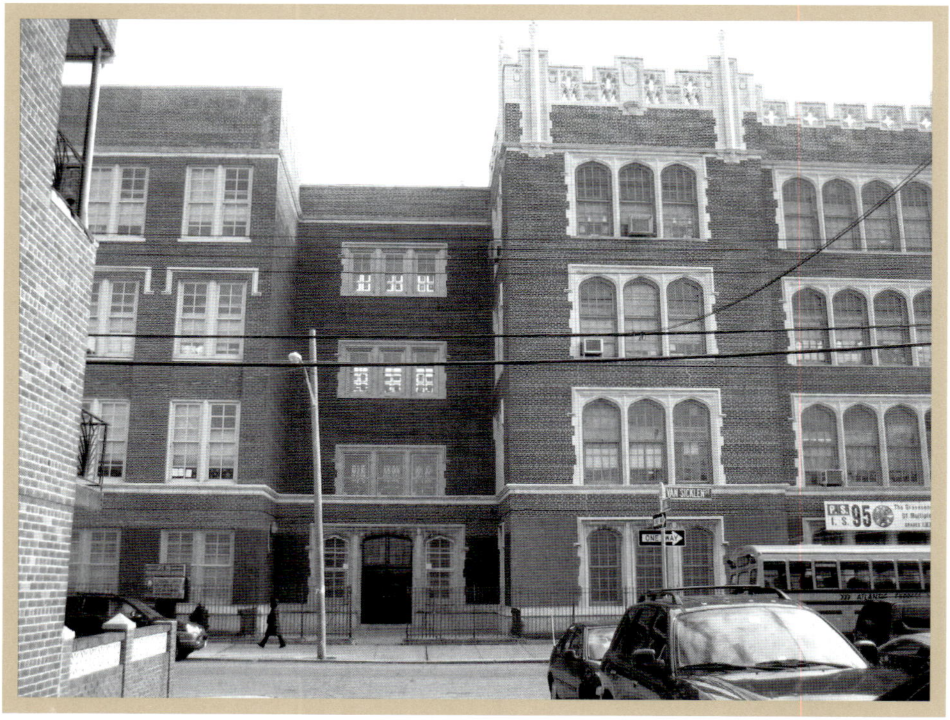

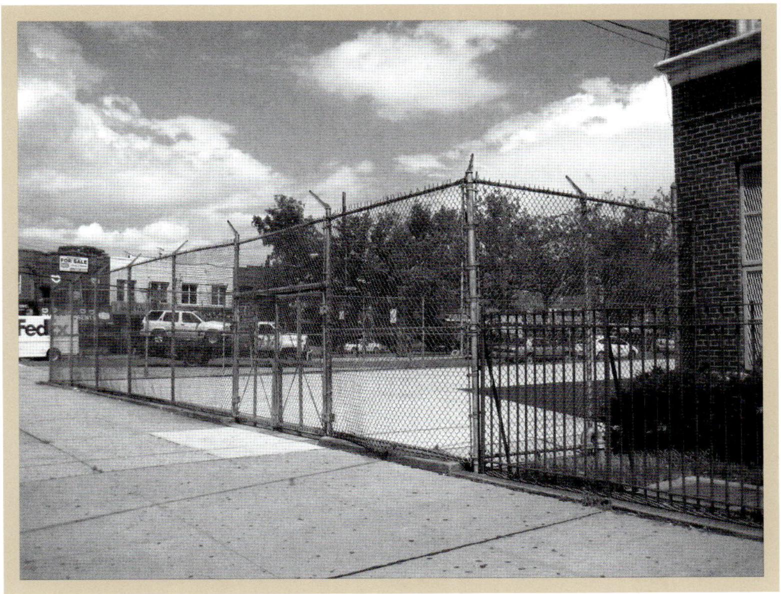

Although not founders of Gravesend, the Van Sicklens arrived earlier than many families. Ferdinando Van Sycklen (about 1635–1712) bought land here in 1669. His descendants lived along their eponymous street into the 20th century. One of their homes, a late-18th- or possibly early-19th-century farmhouse in the typical Dutch style, shown here around 1915, stood at the corner of Van Sicklen Street and Village Road North until 1929, when it was demolished for the schoolyard of P.S. 95.

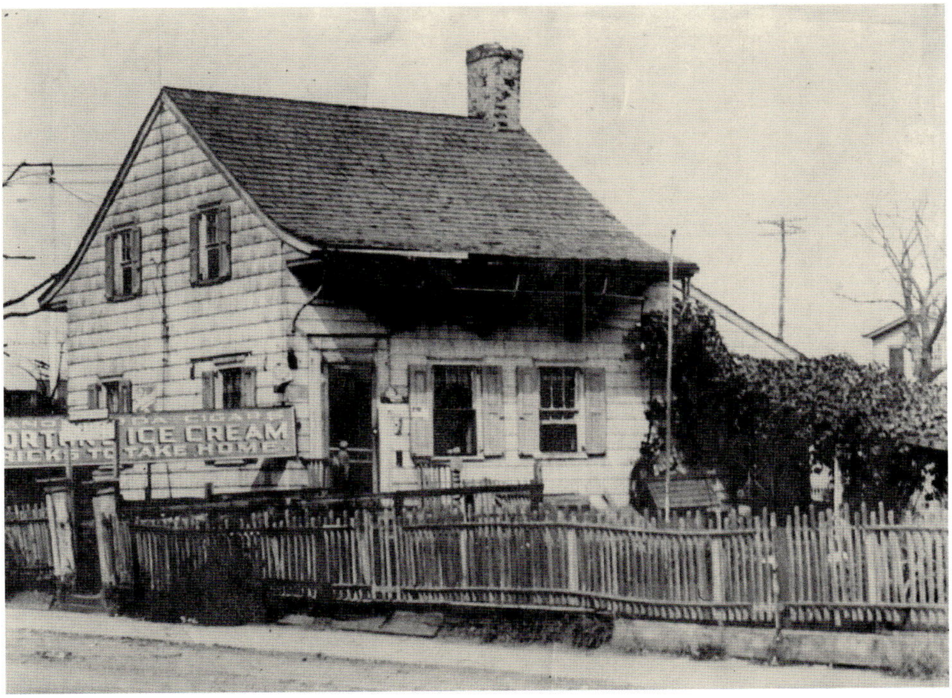

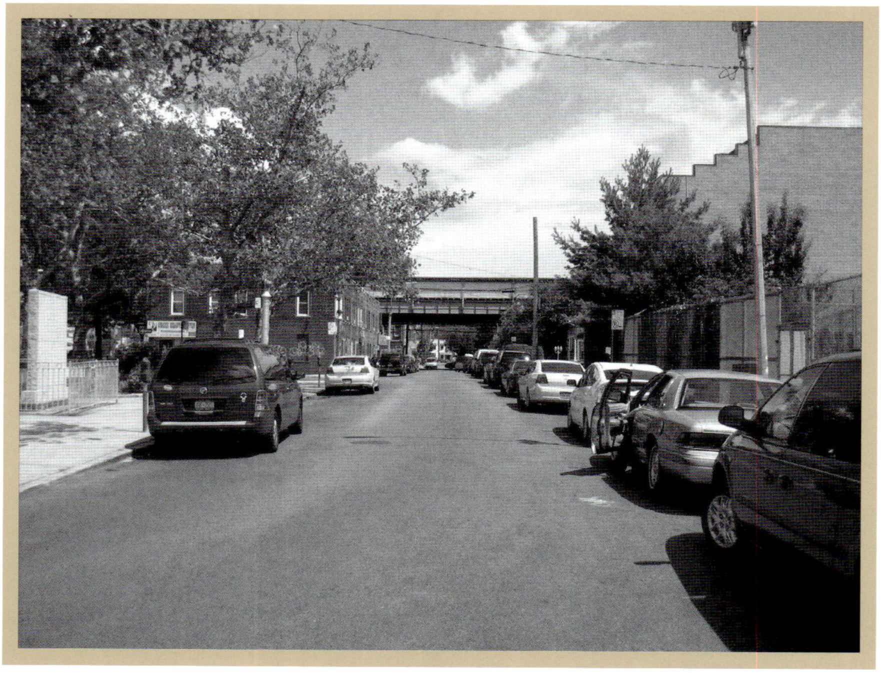

James Hubbard did not name the streets that form the sides of Gravesend's village square when he surveyed them in the 1640s. An 1850s auction advertised property on North Street near West Street, but these labels were not fixed. Some maps join all four streets under the directionless name Village Road. Today's Village Road North, seen here looking east from Van Sicklen Street about 1910, was once called Ryder Place since many Ryder family members lived there.

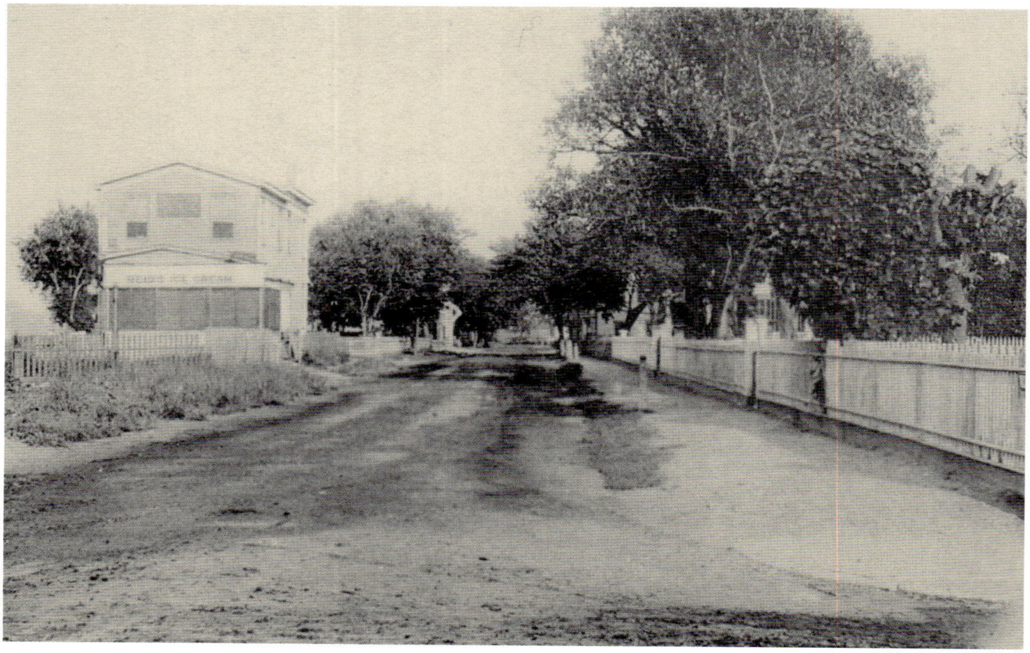

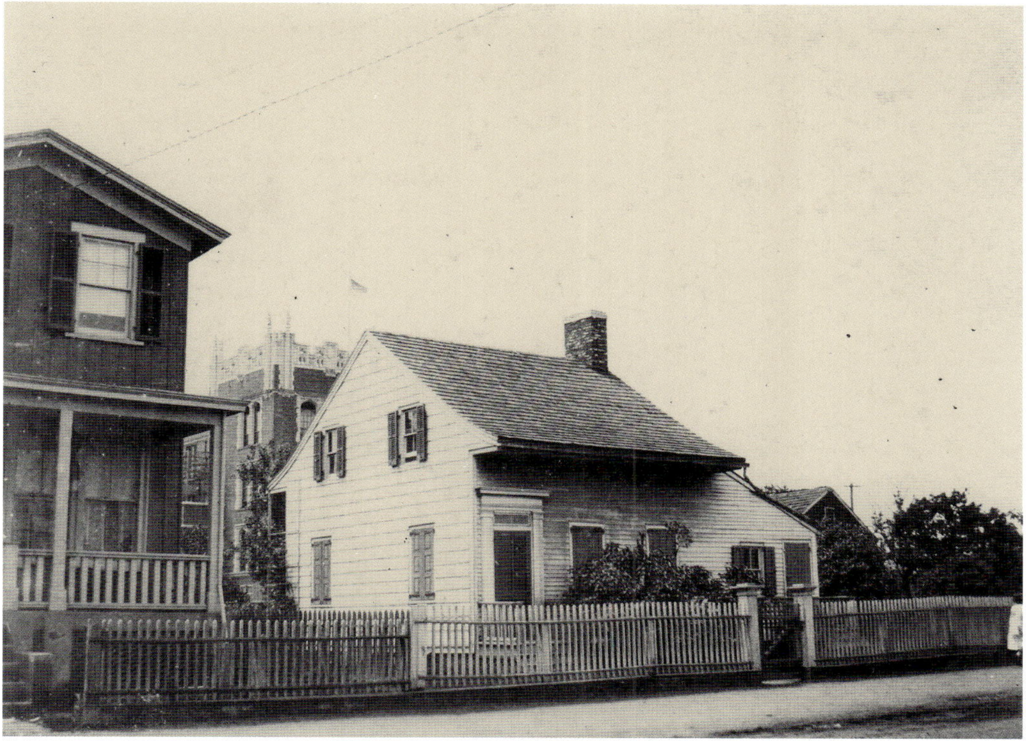

The Dutch-style Ryder–Van Cleef House at 38 Village Road North stood originally at No. 26, where it was built around 1840 by Lawrence Ryder (1809–1863). The marriage of his daughter Maria to John S. Van Cleef gave the house its hyphenated name. It was moved about 100 feet east in 1930 when the city seized its lot for the P.S. 95 schoolyard. The house at left in the 1922 photograph, at 28 Village Road North, was demolished in 2004.

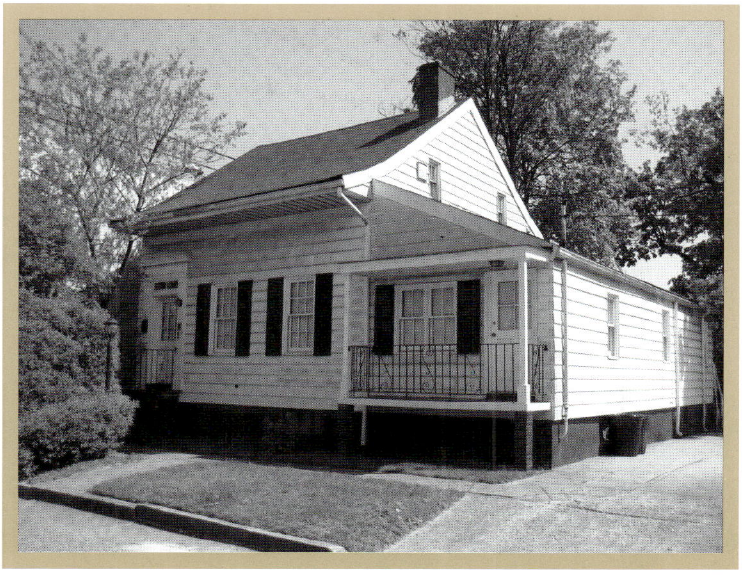

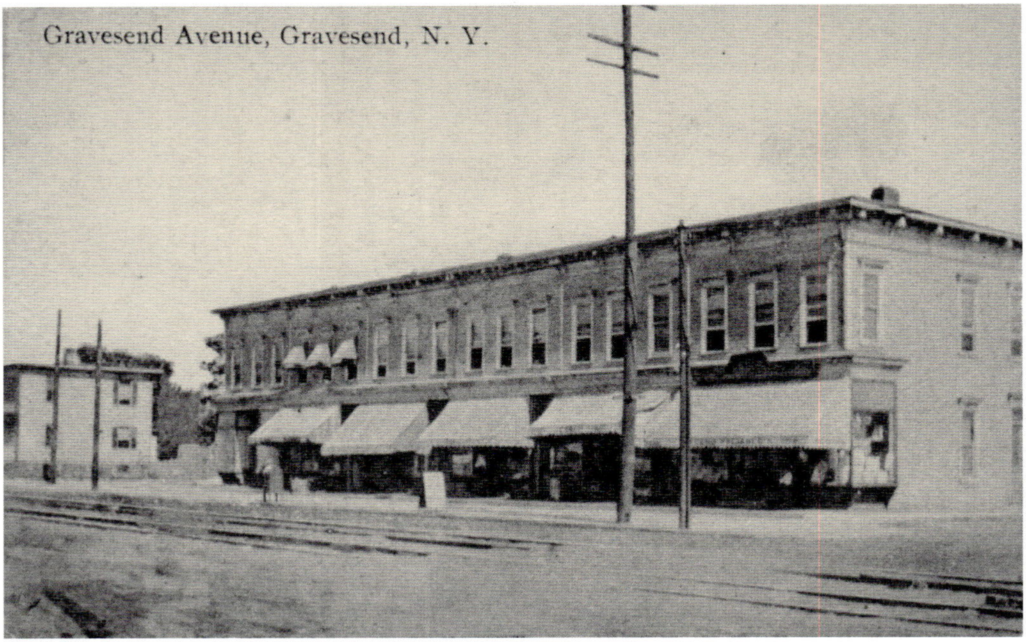

The Culver Line Elevated, today's F train, first rumbled above McDonald Avenue in 1919. About 12 years earlier, the row of flats with ground-floor shops at 2271–2281 went up on the northeast corner of Village Road North. During the 1920s, John Van Kuyk's bakery at 2273 McDonald Avenue (second store from left) catered to Gravesend's Italians, who stopped in craving coffee and buns after fasting for Sunday mass at SS. Simon and Jude Roman Catholic Church.

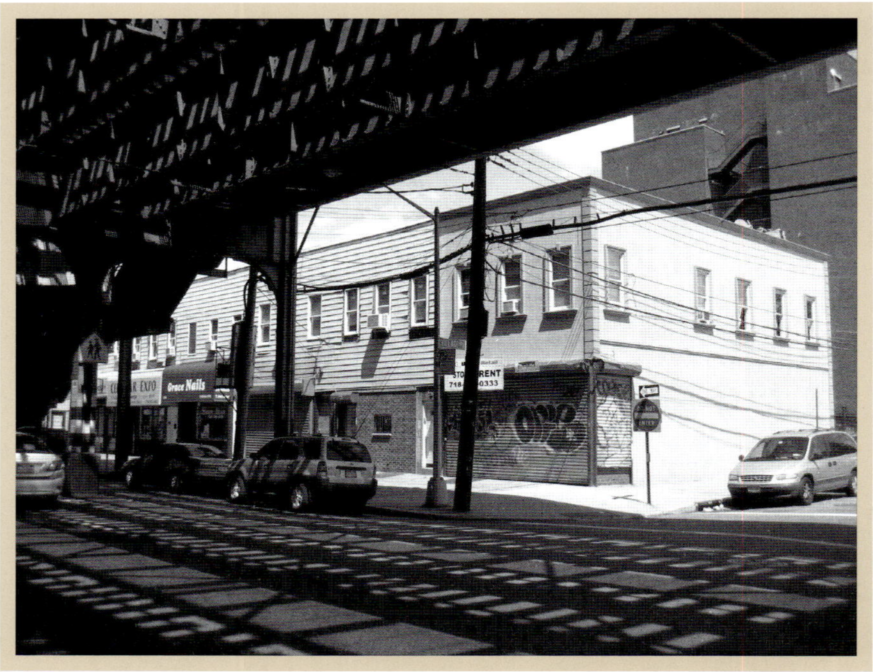

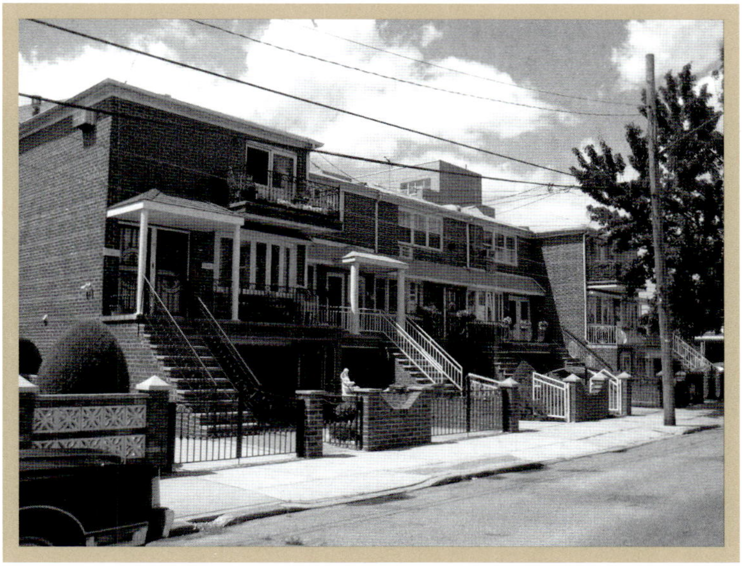

Cornelius and Mary (Van Sicklen) Suydam are seated far right and far left in this *c.* 1910 photograph of their home at 98 Village Road North. They inherited the house from Mary's widowed aunt, whose husband, Stephen J. Stillwell (1836–1882), likely built it around 1857. The Suydams ran an informal garden nursery and each Sunday decorated the Gravesend Reformed Dutch Church with colorful blooms. Their house was demolished about 1971 for the brick row numbered 6–14 Village Road East.

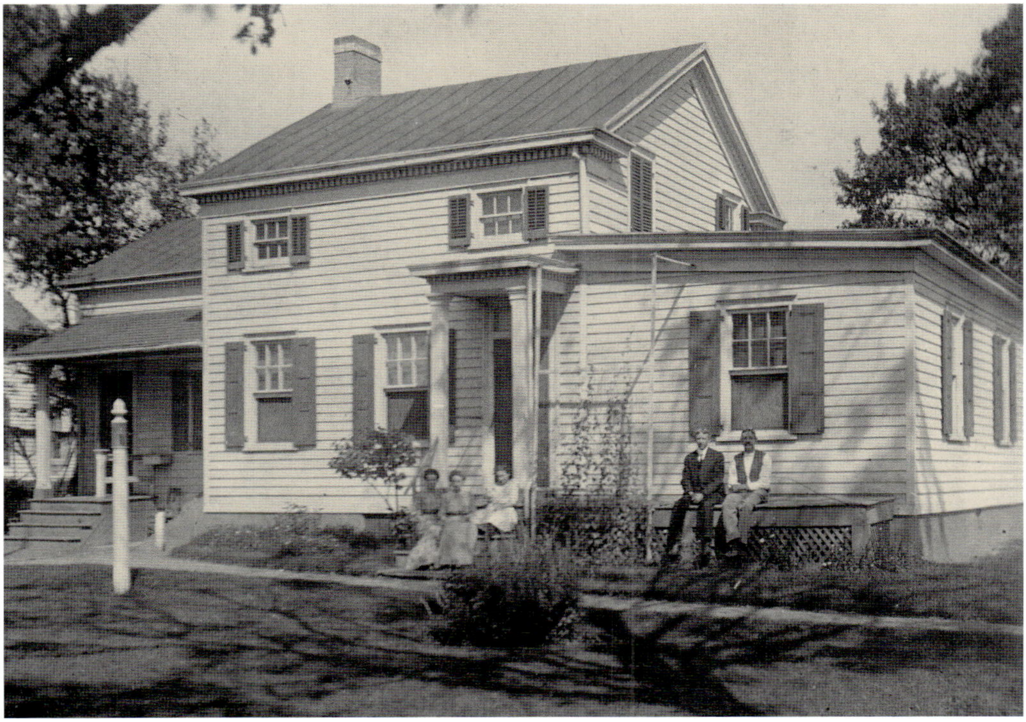

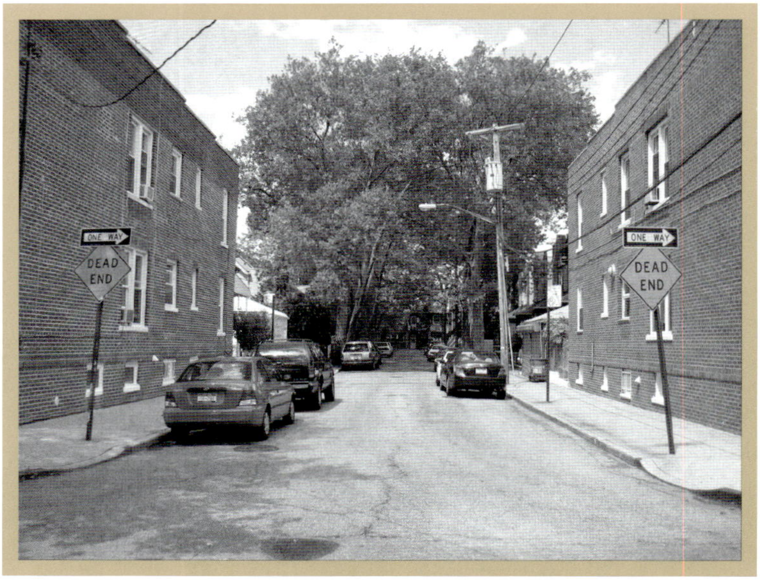

Like Corso Court off Van Sicklen Street, Village Court—the cul-de-sac built about 1930 off Village Road South—also replaced a Dutch farmhouse. The 1780 Williamson house was the centerpiece of a vast property that stretched southeast to Ocean Parkway and Avenue Z. Around 1902, Stephen Stryker Williamson (1840–1913) sold the farmland, which his family owned since 1665, to the realtors Wood, Harmon and Company, who developed it as South Marlboro.

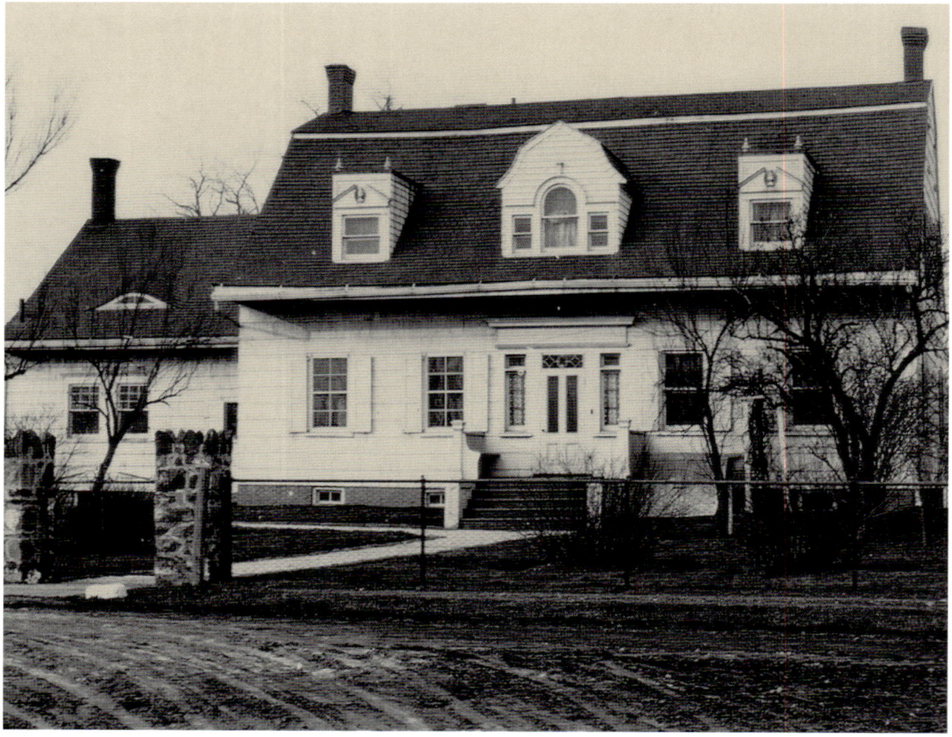

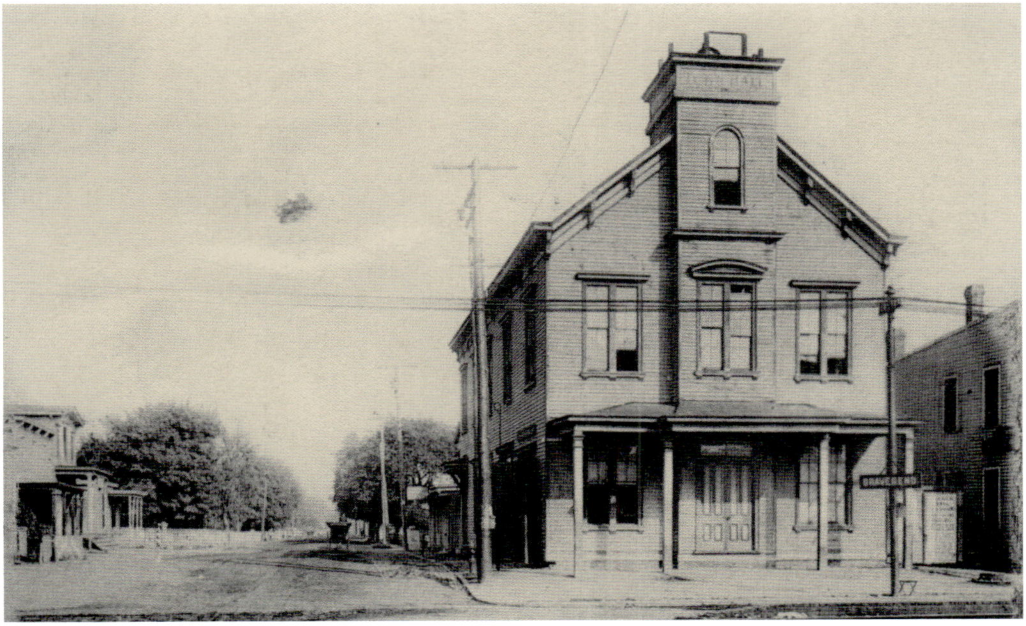

Gravesend's town hall at 2337 McDonald Avenue replaced a 1788 schoolhouse (supposedly where George Washington visited on April 20, 1790), which was moved and now stands at 32 Village Road North. The new structure, seen here around 1910, was built in 1873 and held an auditorium, courtroom, and four basement jail cells. After the City of Brooklyn annexed Gravesend in 1894, the building housed the predecessor of today's Fire Engine Company 254. It was demolished in 1913.

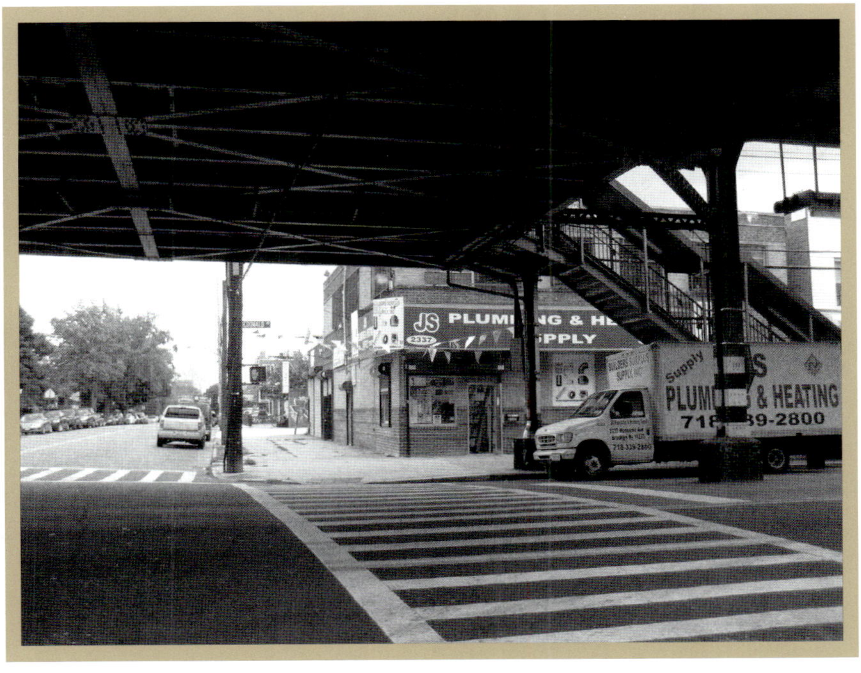

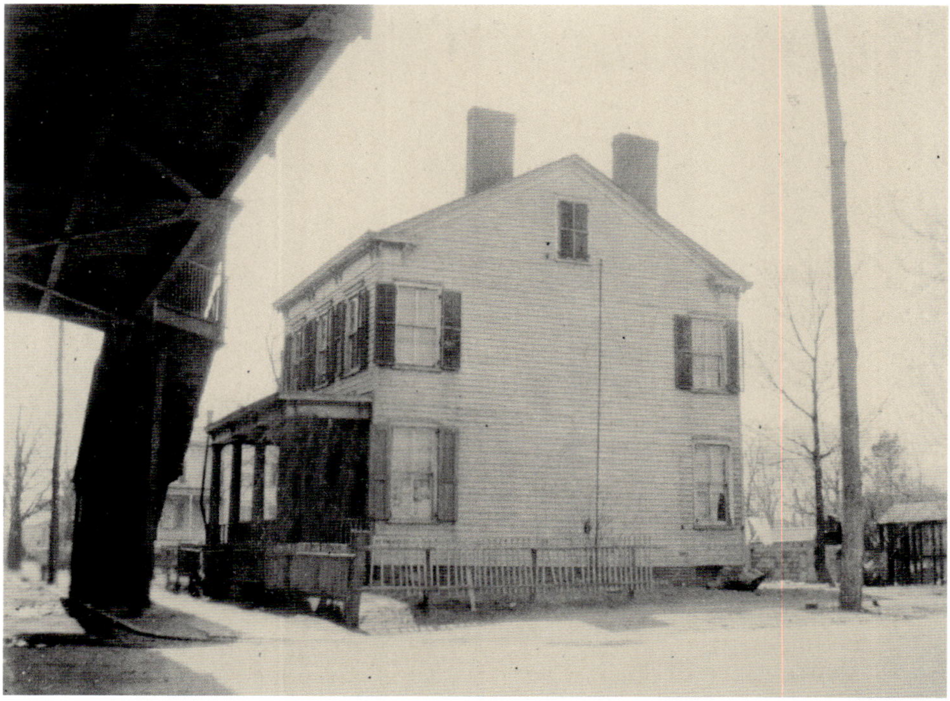

Samuel Hubbard (1812–1900), a descendant of Gravesend patentee James Hubbard, is usually linked to the 1830s farmhouse on page 73. Just before 1861, he built this house at 2338 McDonald Avenue. It was here on June 18, 1878, that his wife, Maria Louisa, swallowed a lethal glass of strychnine-laced beer. The coroner's inquest found Samuel had poisoned her, but a grand jury failed to indict for murder. Husband and wife lie buried together in the Gravesend Cemetery.

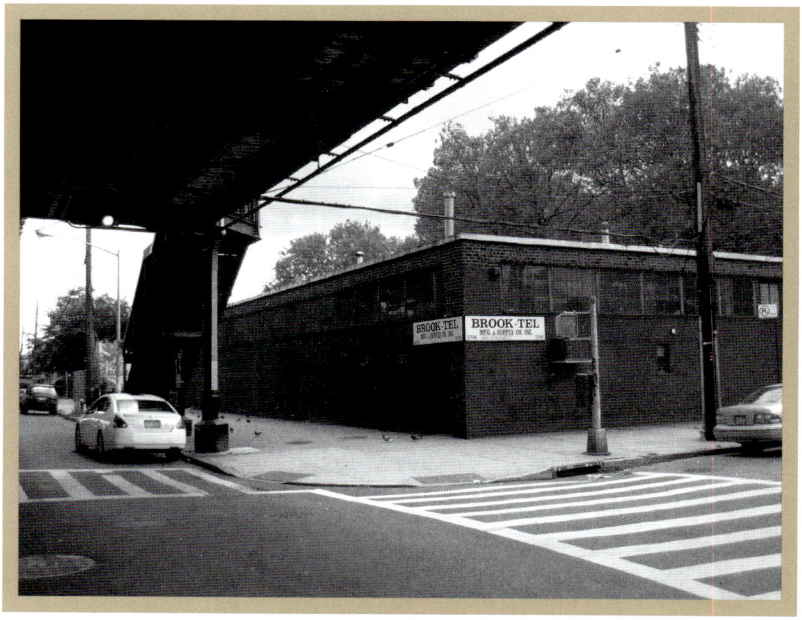

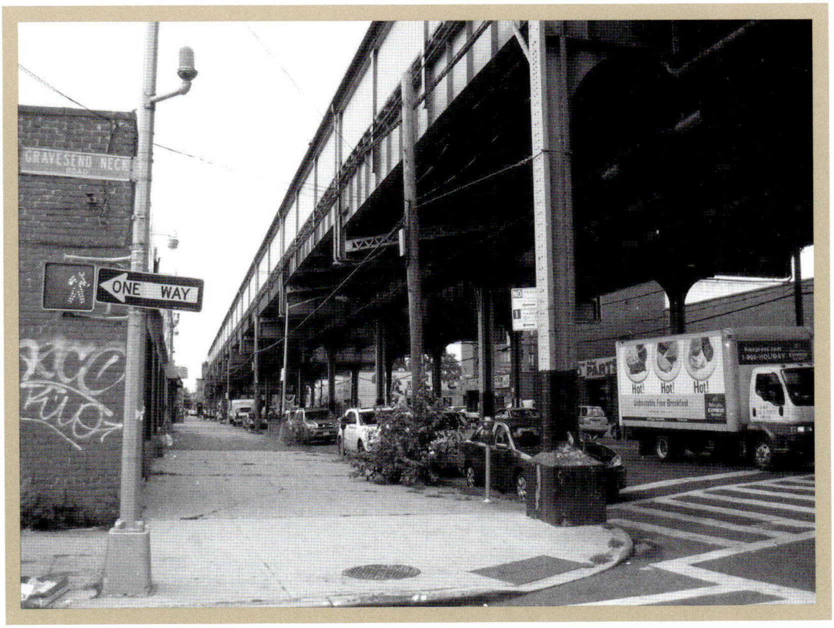

Despite a court ruling that the collection of two fares for a trip to Coney Island was illegal, on August 12, 1906, the Brooklyn Rapid Transit (BRT) Company demanded a second nickel from trolley riders once they passed Kings Highway. The BRT's uniformed "police" ejected every passenger who refused to pay. One girl fell into Coney Island Creek and drowned. An unidentified photographer (possibly Edwin Levick) caught the day's mayhem looking north on McDonald Avenue from Gravesend Neck Road.

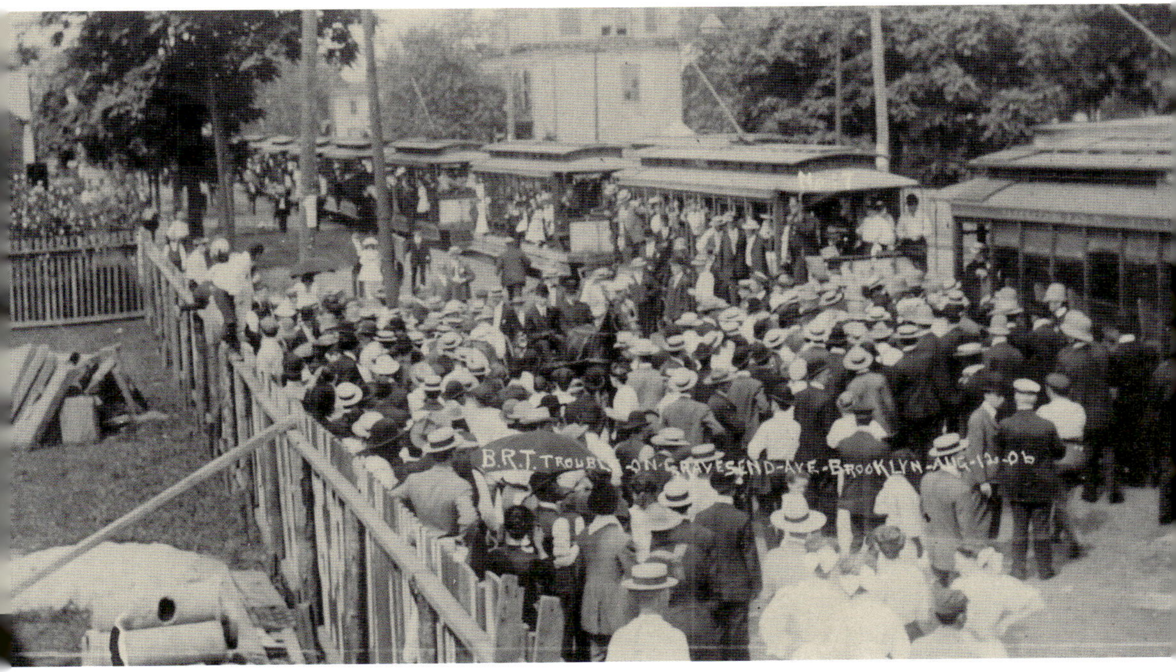

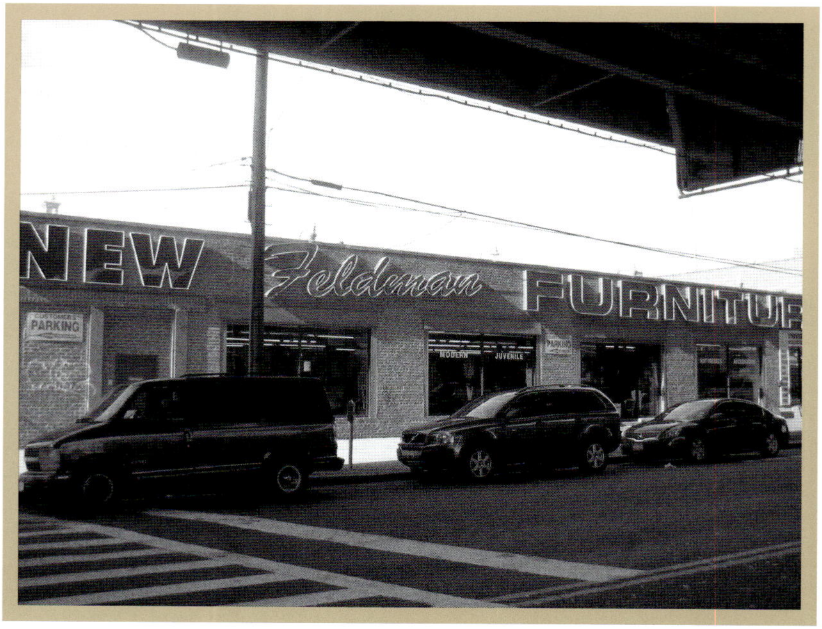

Between 1667 and 1833, the Gravesend Reformed Dutch Church met in various buildings on the west side of McDonald Avenue north of Gravesend Neck Road. The church seen here (behind the trees) was dedicated in 1834. The adjacent Sunday school was built about 1854. Railroad traffic eventually made the site undesirable. The church was demolished in 1893 and the Sunday school was moved three blocks east to house services while the sanctuary on page 38 was under construction.

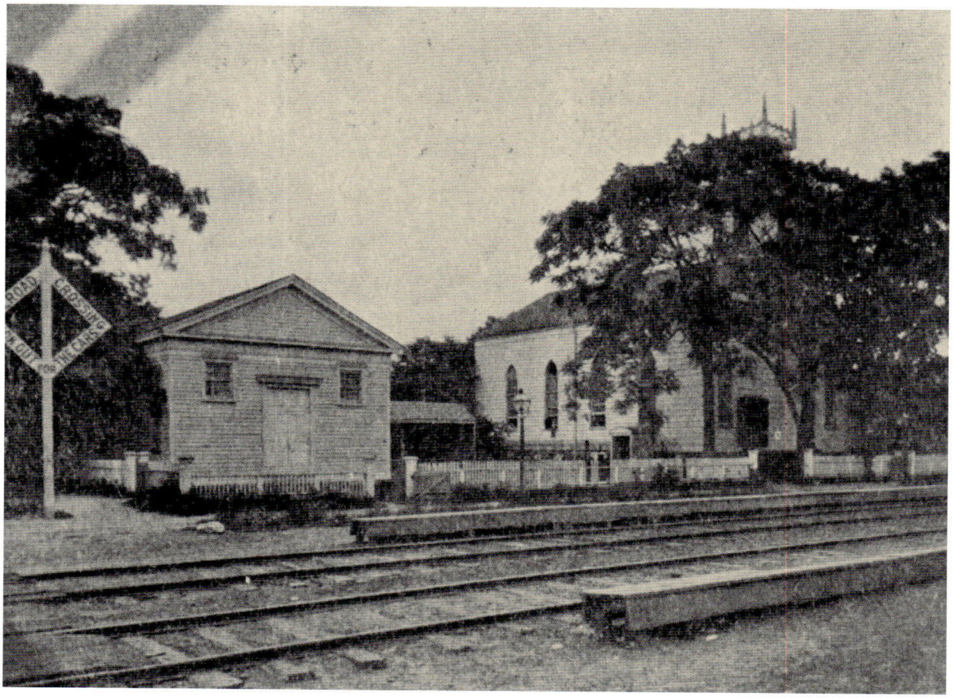

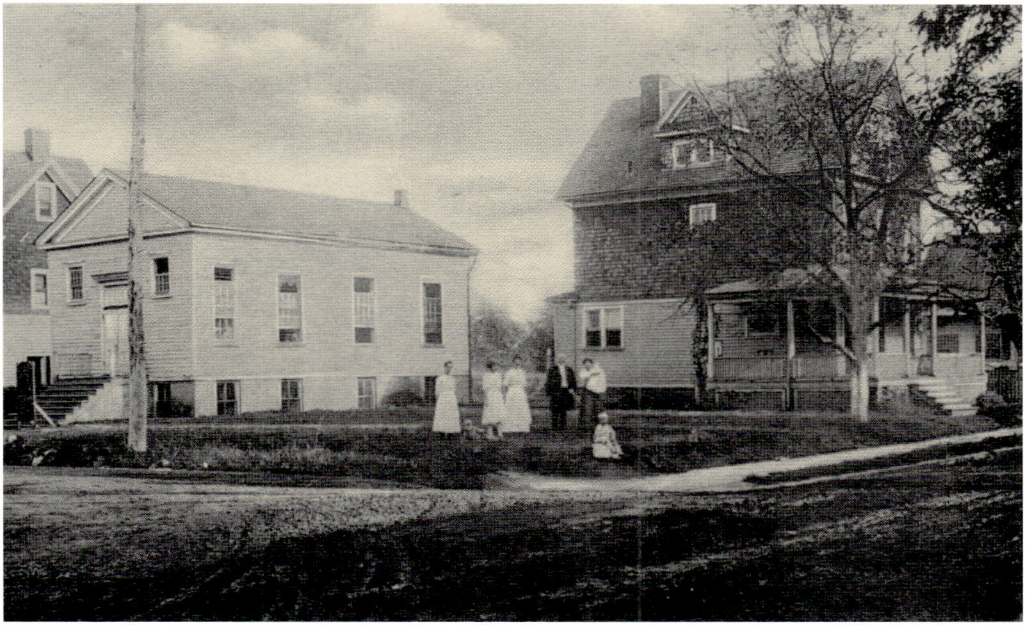

The old Sunday school of the Gravesend Reformed Dutch Church became superfluous once the new sanctuary on page 38 was complete. In 1899, it was sold to the fledgling Gravesend Methodist Episcopal Church and moved—for the second time in six years—to 14 Gravesend Neck Road. After that congregation dissolved in 1914, the building housed the Coney Island Pentecostal Church, which replaced it in 1937 with the current stone structure. It is now the First Korean Church of Brooklyn.

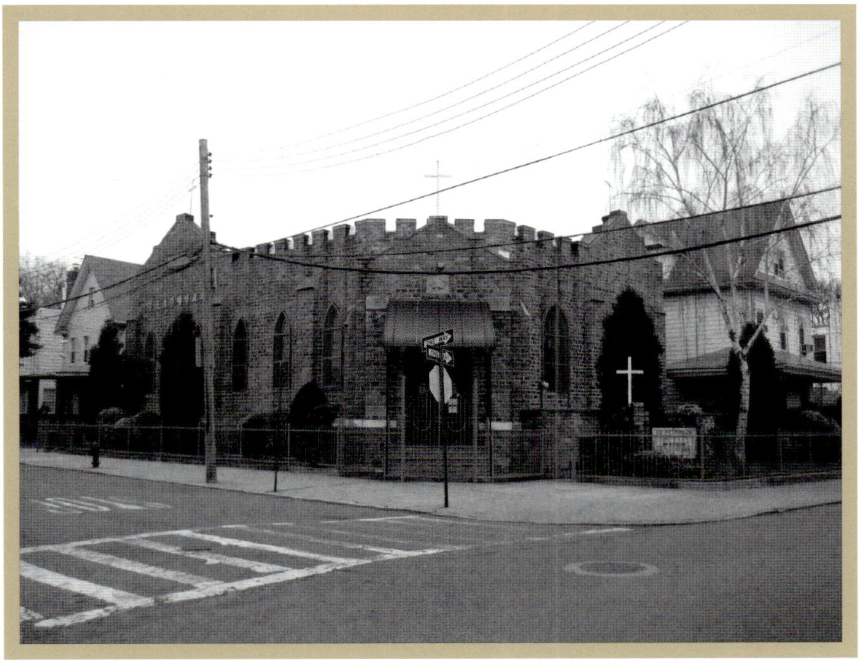

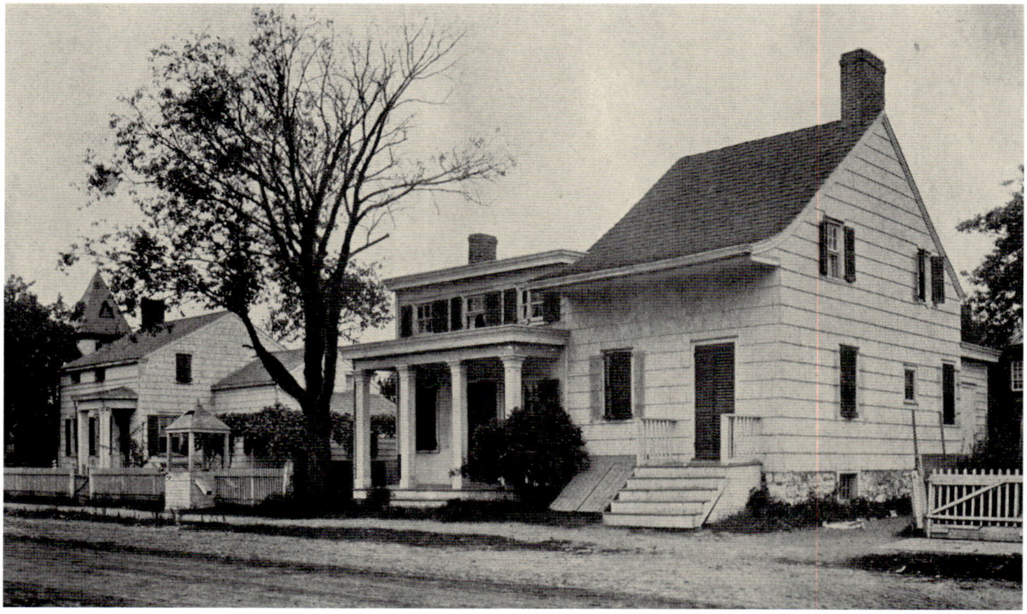

The 19th-century Donly house on the north side of Gravesend Neck Road at Van Sicklen Street (left of the tree in the 1910 photograph) was demolished to build the 1915 portion of P.S. 95. The neighboring 18th-century Wiltse house at 15–17 Gravesend Neck Road—in the ubiquitous Dutch style with a later Greek Revival addition—escaped immediate destruction, but came down around 1930 for expansion of the schoolyard.

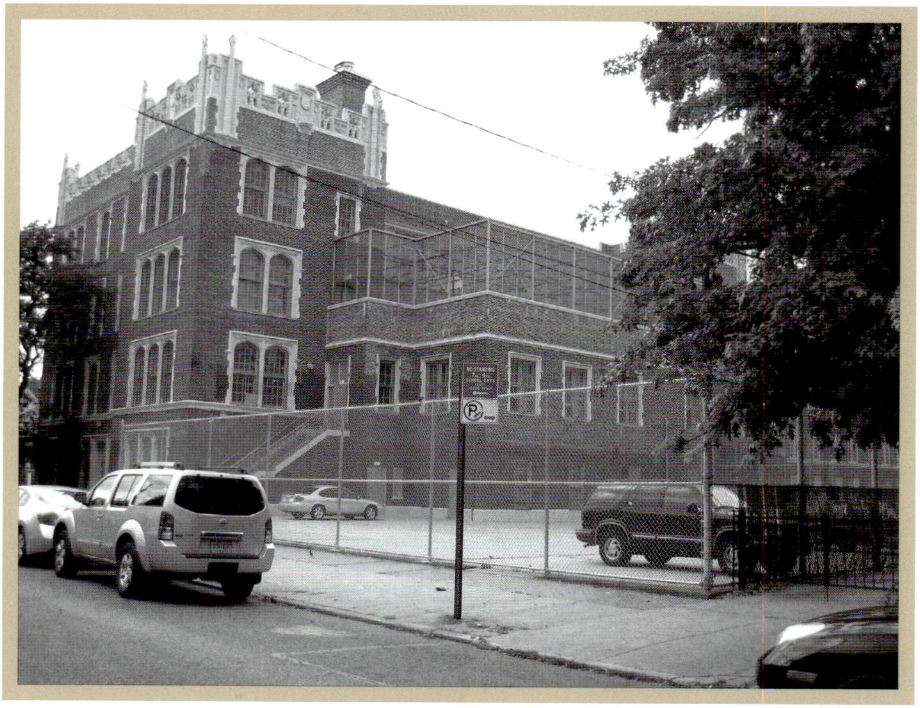

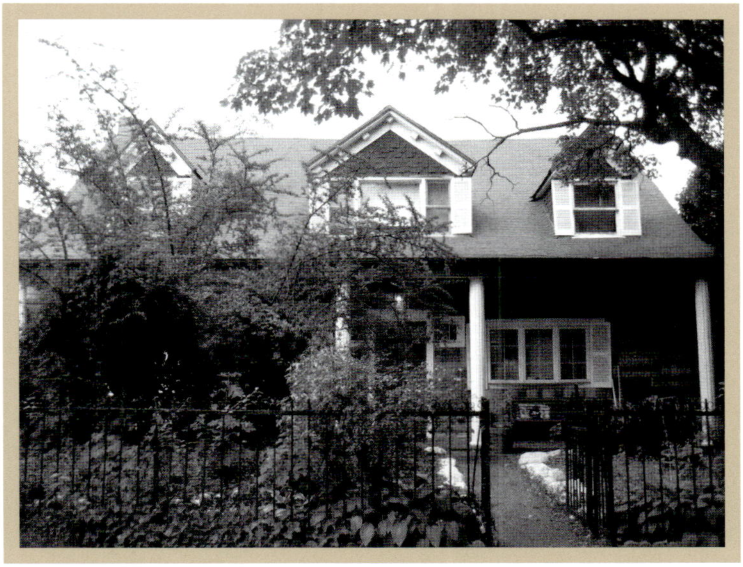

The construction date of the house at 27 Gravesend Neck Road is in perpetual dispute. Once home to the Van Sicklen and Hicks families, it was sold to William and Isabelle Platt who called it the Lady Moody Homestead, a misnomer that has stuck since 1909. Although it stands on land originally owned by Moody, its flared Dutch eaves are more common on structures built after her lifetime (she died around 1659). Whatever its precise age, the house remains the oldest in Gravesend.

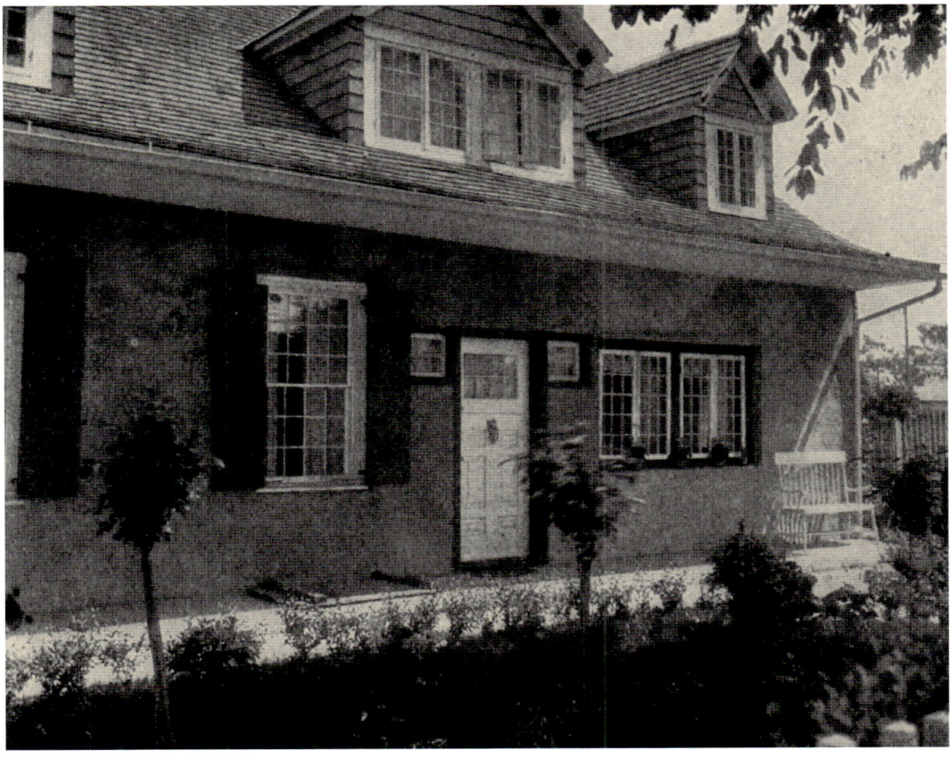

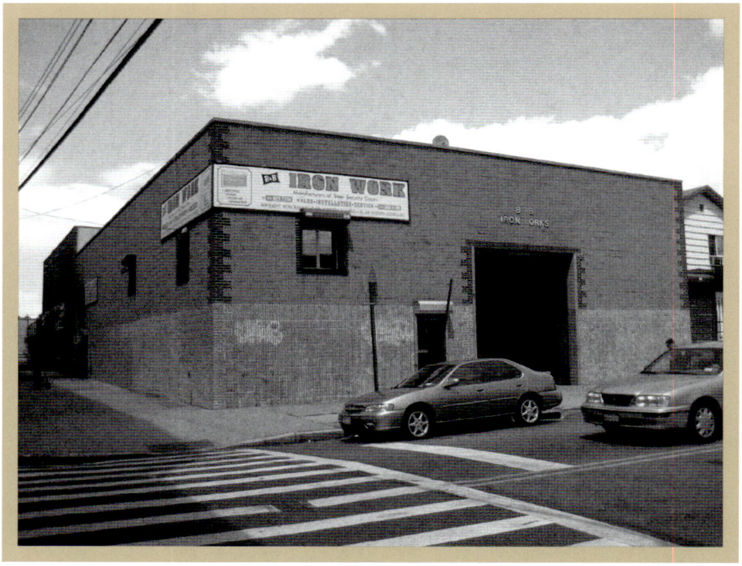

No. 51 Gravesend Neck Road was a small hotel sited strategically at the northeast corner of McDonald Avenue, steps from the railroad tracks and opposite the town hall and church. Once run by renowned horseman Simeon D. Hoagland (1817–1897), the hotel passed to German immigrant Christian Heerlein, whose widow, Catharine, managed it after 1887 while her son, Louis, tended bar. By 1905, E. Ackermann had become proprietor of the Old Gravesend Inn. It stood until the 1950s.

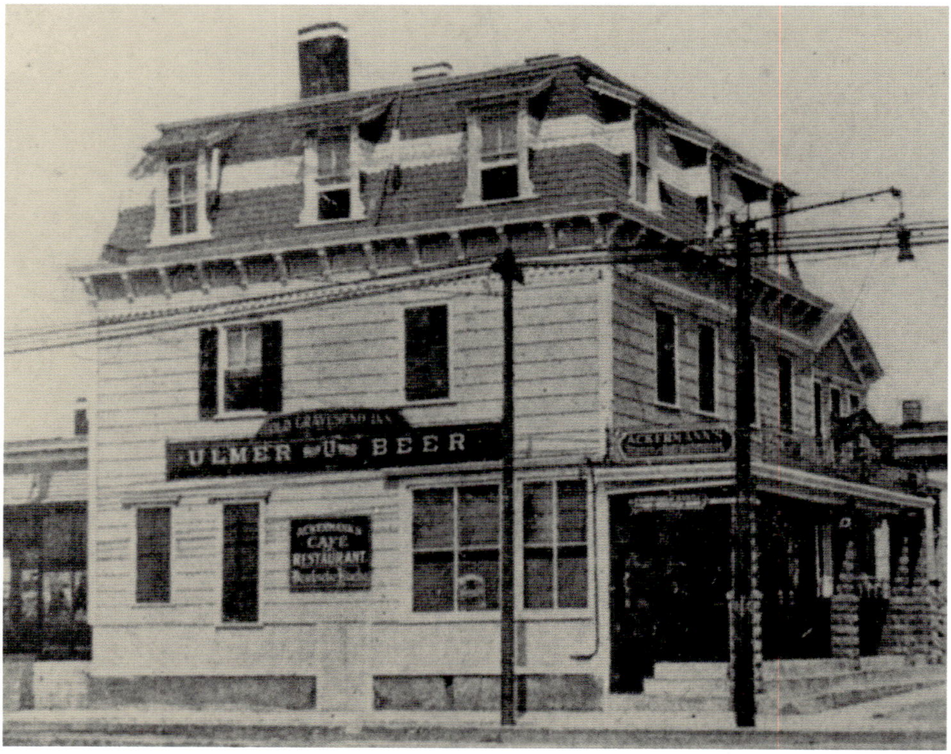

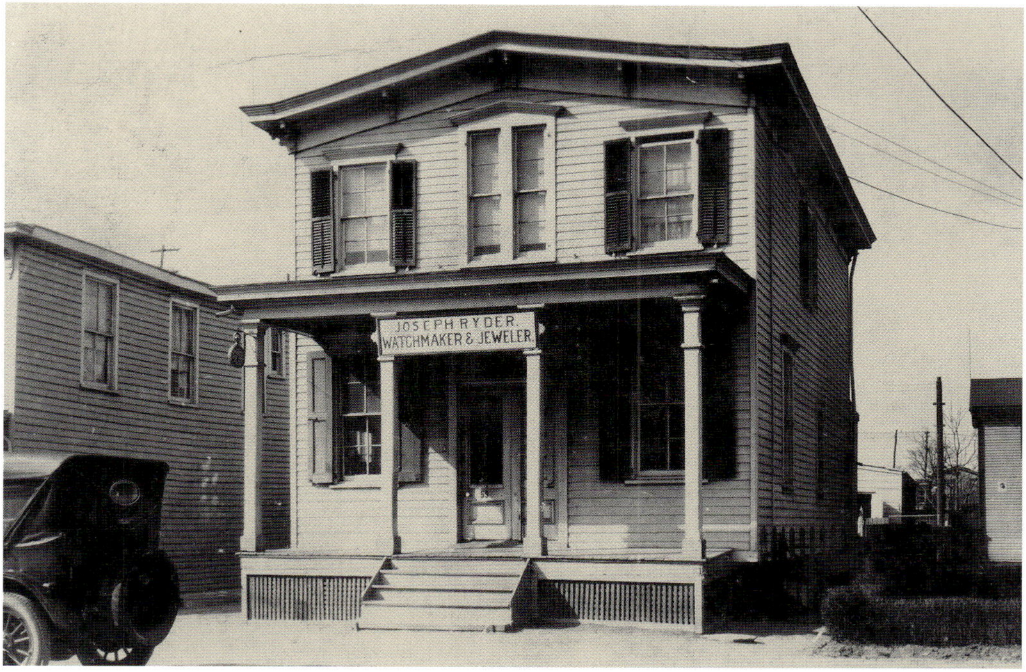

No. 59 Gravesend Neck Road was home to German immigrants Joseph and Justina (Asenbauer) Ryder (originally spelled Reiter and no relation to the early Gravesend Ryder family). Joseph (1857–1928) was a jeweler who kept shop in the left front parlor. Justina (about 1864–1932) was a busy midwife who delivered some 1,200 babies between 1890 and 1913 (the years recorded in her surviving journal). Their house was demolished in December 2007. (Courtesy of Albert C. Simmel Jr.)

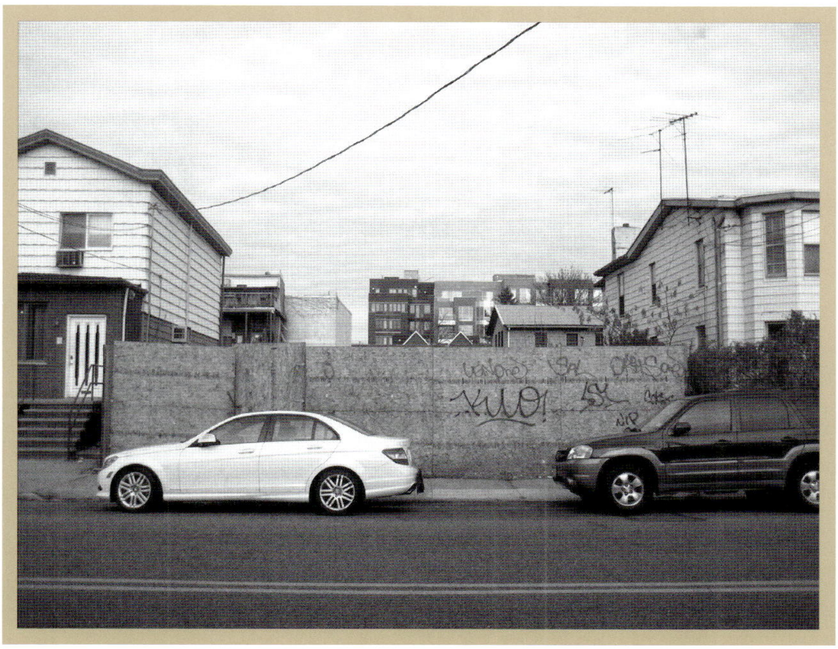

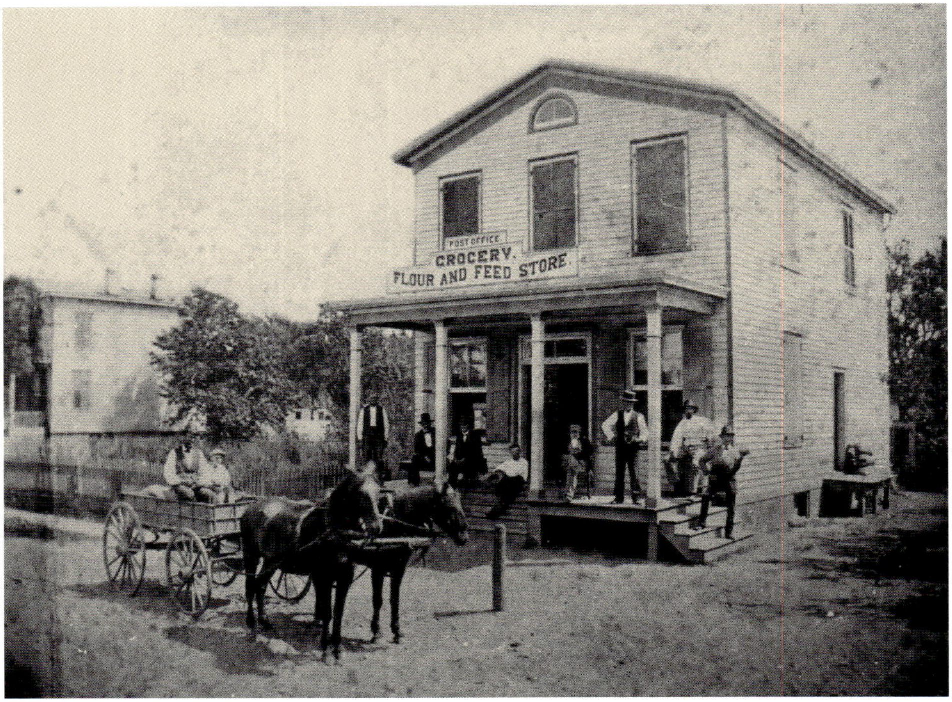

Before 1843, mail destined for sparsely populated Gravesend went to nearby Flatbush, where any farmer passing by collected it for his neighbors. Gravesend's first postmaster, Martin Schoonmaker, who served from 1843 to 1854, kept office in his store on McDonald Avenue. Later this grocery at 66 Gravesend Neck Road also doubled as the post office. Small town residents, like these men gathered on the porch to socialize, spread news faster by word of mouth than it traveled by letter.

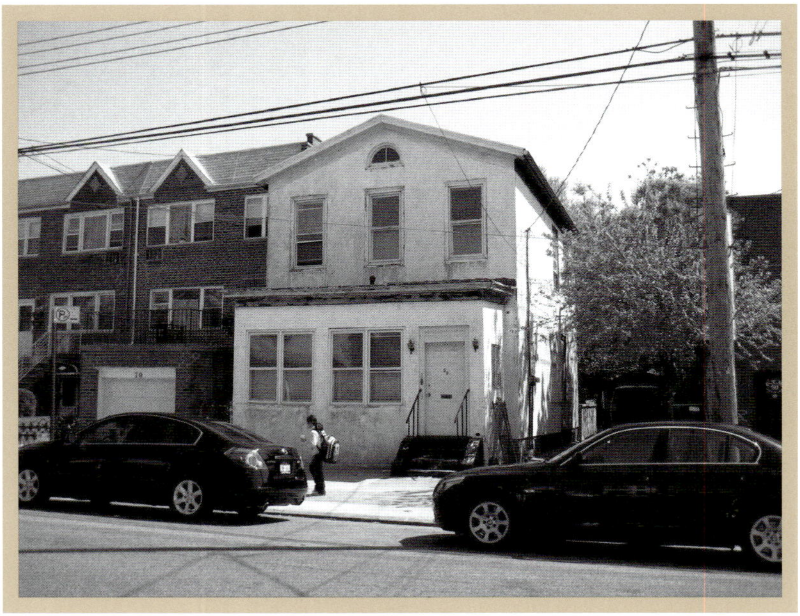

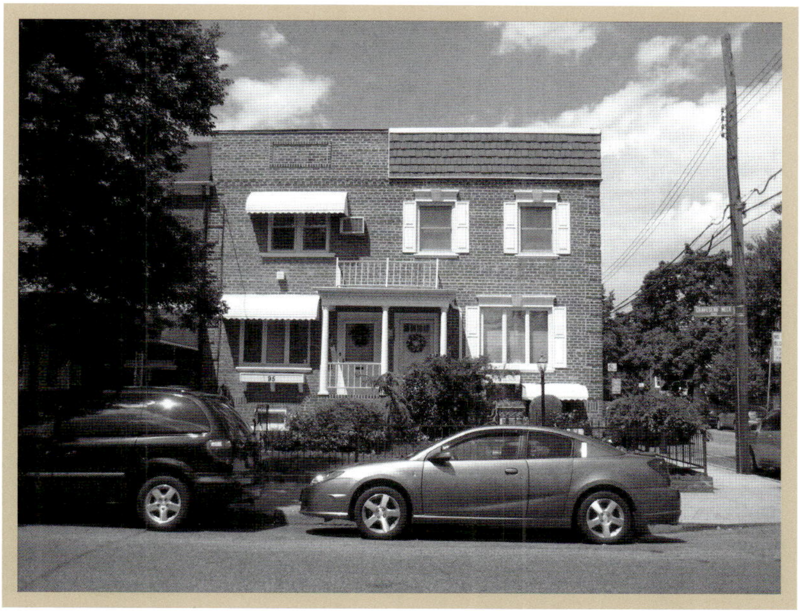

The Emmons family built the picturesque Dutch farmhouse at 95 Gravesend Neck Road around 1800. Eventually it passed to a descendant, the watchcase maker John M. Stillwell (1821–1903). Stillwell's son-in-law and heir Frederick E. H. Renaud (1855–1930) shared his profession, but abandoned it to study medicine. Some members of the nearby Gravesend Reformed Dutch Church shunned Dr. Renaud for his sacrilegious habit of pulling weeds on Sunday. His home and garden, seen here in 1913, were gone by 1937.

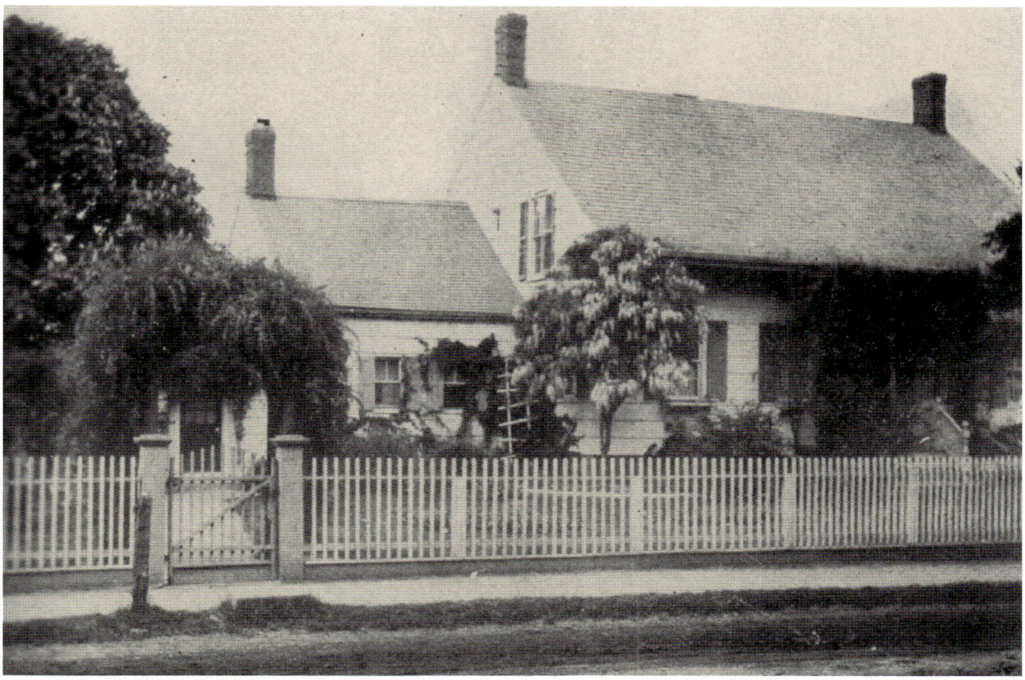

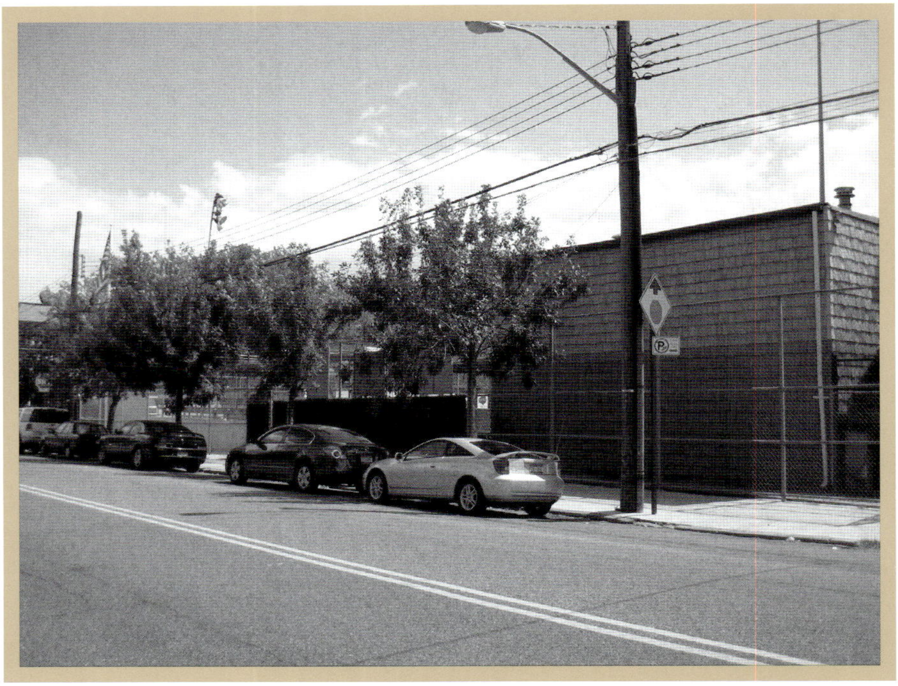

The Greek Revival–style house with Italianate details at 102 Gravesend Neck Road was built by the prosperous farmer Daniel Stillwell (1797–1863). His youngest daughter, Elizabeth (1837–1911), inherited the house and in later years occupied it with one servant. On her death she left it to her seamstress, Mary Bennett (1856–1931). That was no small gift: by 1930 the house was worth $35,000. Eventually it fell into disrepair and was demolished for the present athletic field in 1956.

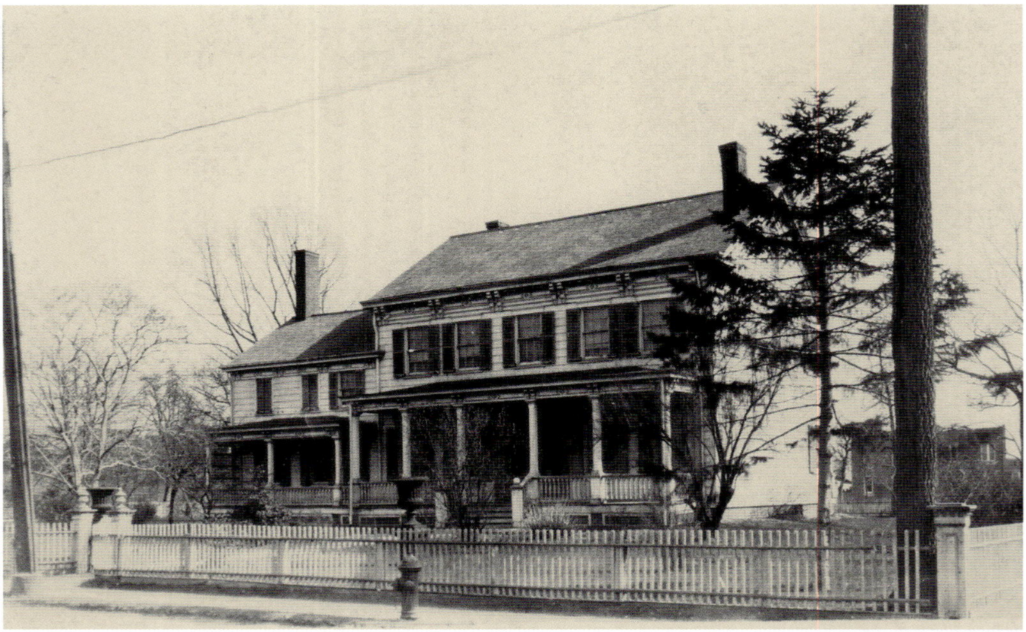

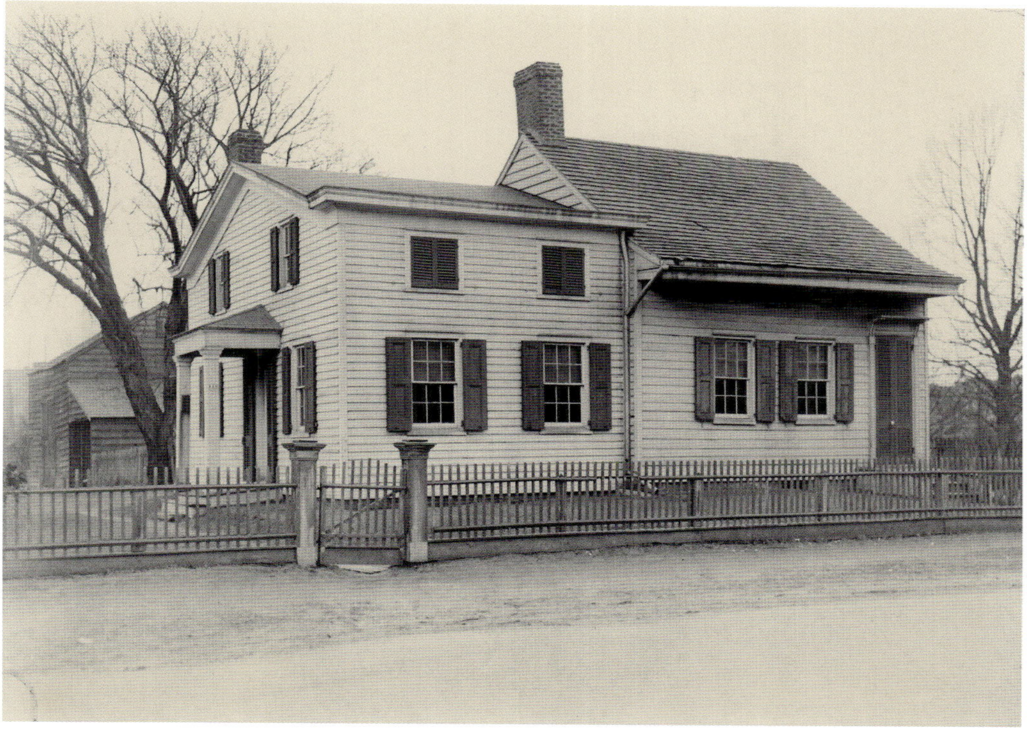

Abraham Emmons (1809–1832) built the Dutch (right) half of 110 Gravesend Neck Road before 1831. His son, another Abraham Emmons (1833–1931), added the oddly juxtaposed extension after 1863. Marie M. Moore (born 1914), a member during the 1920s of the Gravesend Reformed Dutch Church across the street, recalls that the farmhouse "had no electricity or running water" and how "Old Abraham" tilled his fields "using a hand plow and a horse." His house disappeared between 1945 and 1956.

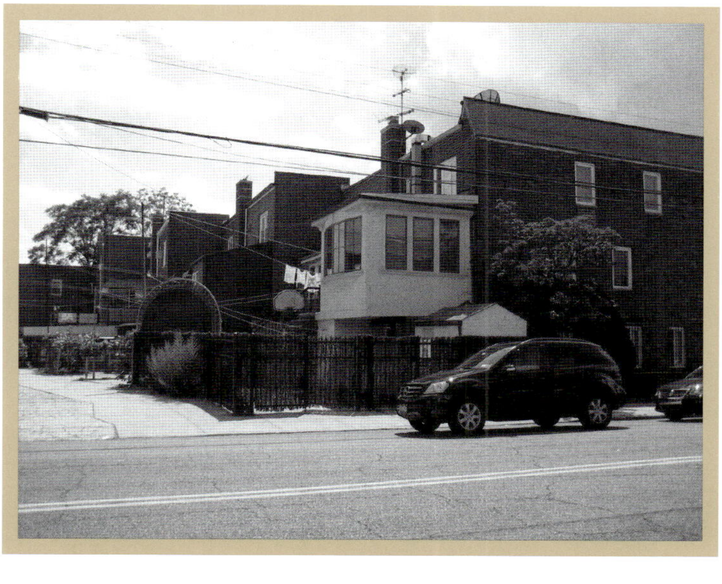

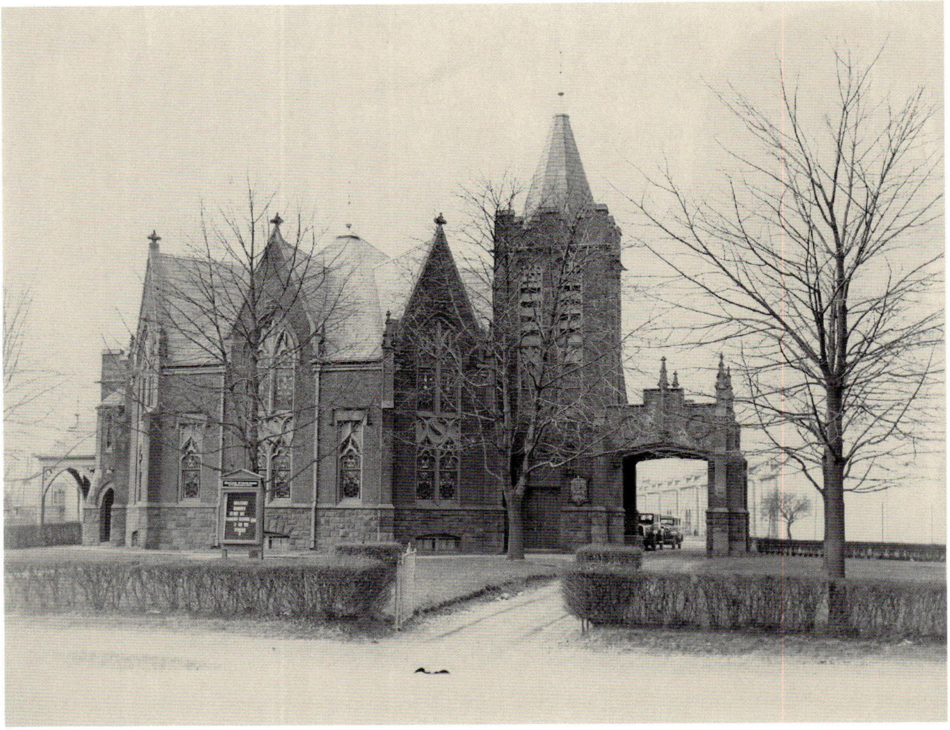

After the Gravesend Reformed Dutch Church abandoned its home near the railroad tracks in 1893, it built this imposing neo-Gothic sanctuary at 121 Gravesend Neck Road with architect J. Graham Glover, completing it in 1894. In 1979, the dwindling congregation federated with the Advent Lutheran Church at 1209 Avenue P, moving there as the interdenominational Advent-Gravesend Church. The Coney Island Pentecostal Church bought 121 Gravesend Neck Road, moved in, and rechristened it the Trinity Tabernacle of Gravesend.

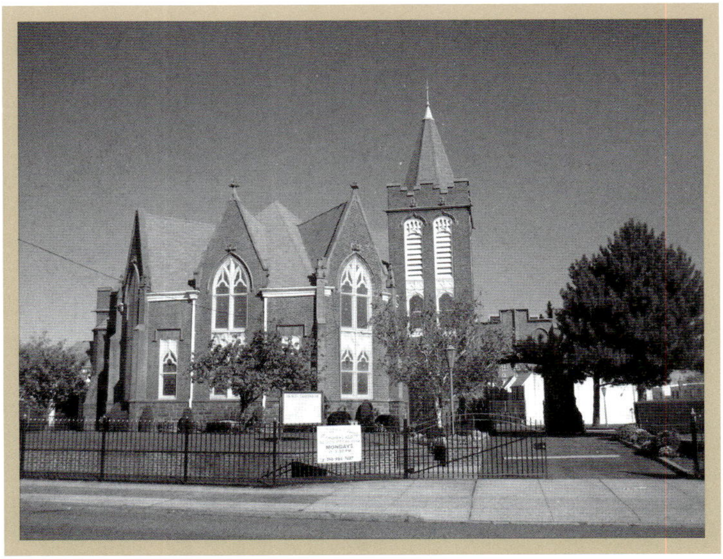

CHAPTER 2

Eastern Gravesend

Homecrest, Sheepshead Bay, and Marine Park

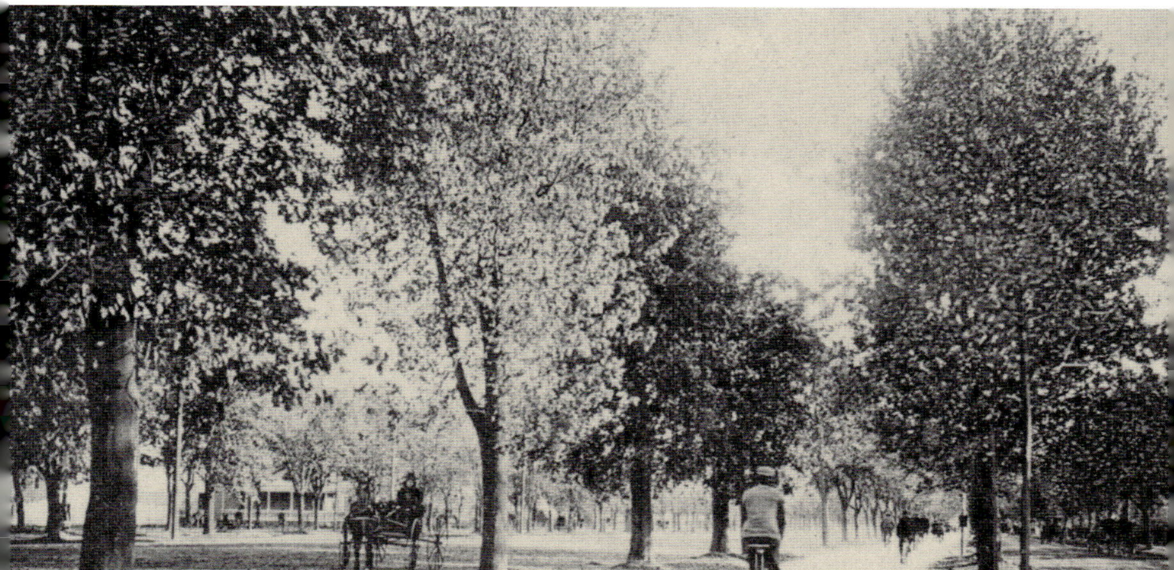

Ocean Parkway runs nearly six miles between Prospect Park and Coney Island. Constructed in 1874–1876 by Frederick Law Olmsted and Calvert Vaux (who created Central Park), this first planned parkway in America became a scenic landmark in 1975. Two half-mile stones survive along its western mall: "3/M" south of Avenue P and "5/M" at the northwest corner of Neptune Avenue.

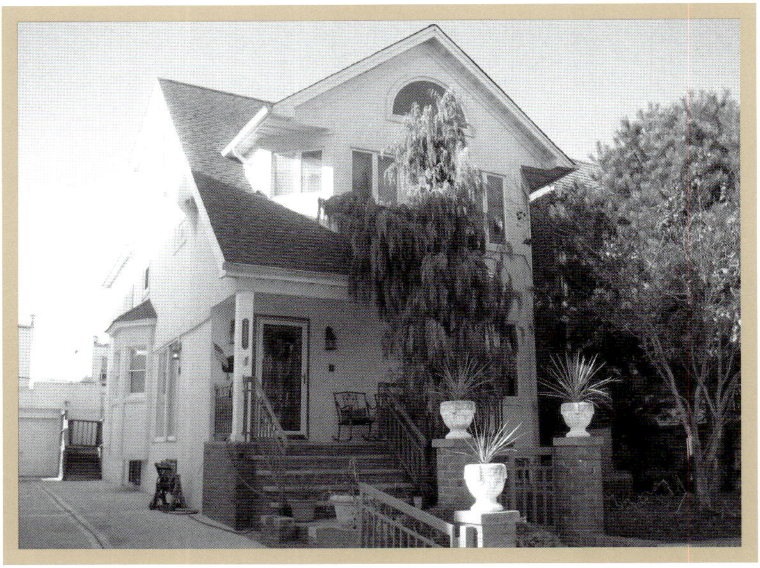

Beginning in 1903, one could buy land at South Marlboro, the Wood, Harmon and Company development on the former Williamson farm, southeast of Gravesend's village square. Single lots (20 by 100 feet) on side streets began at $490; those on avenues sold only in pairs from $520 each. Ocean Parkway frontages started at $800 and triple-lot corners at $2,020. No. 2350 East Second Street was built on a double lot around 1904. (Courtesy of the New-York Historical Society.)

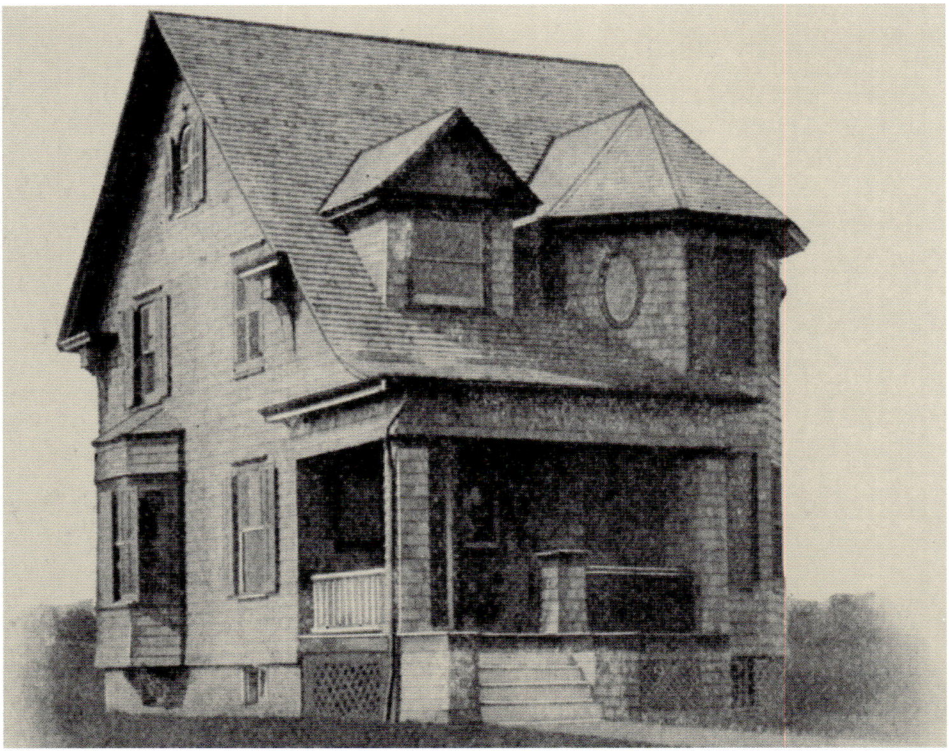

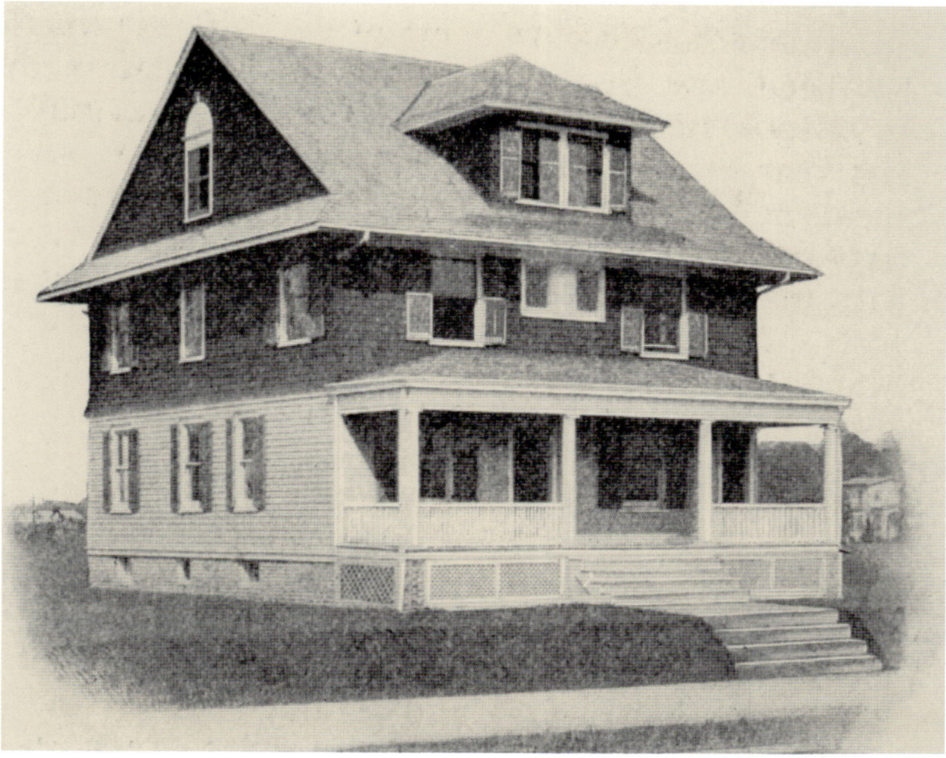

Wood, Harmon and Company advertised in 1903 how South Marlboro would be "improved in our usual perfect manner, with macadamized streets, granolithic sidewalks and curbs, fine shade trees and shrubbery." Despite these slightly grandiose promises, the development never attracted much significant or uniform housing construction. A few residences went up late in 1904, like this one at 365 Avenue W, but the surrounding lots remained scrubby and largely vacant well into the 1920s. (Courtesy of the New-York Historical Society.)

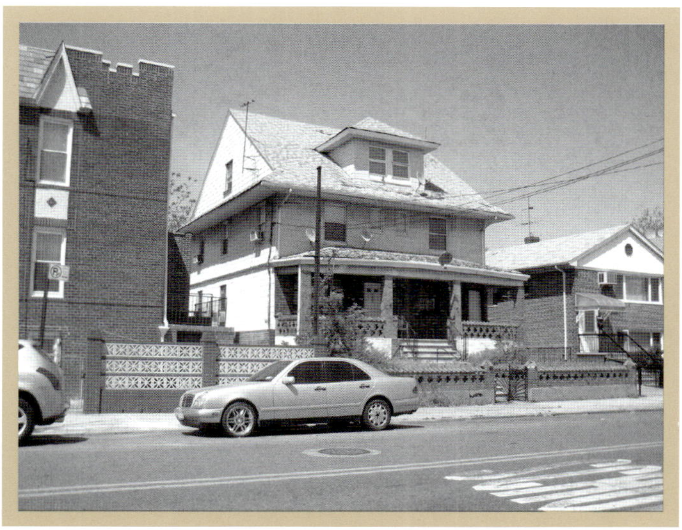

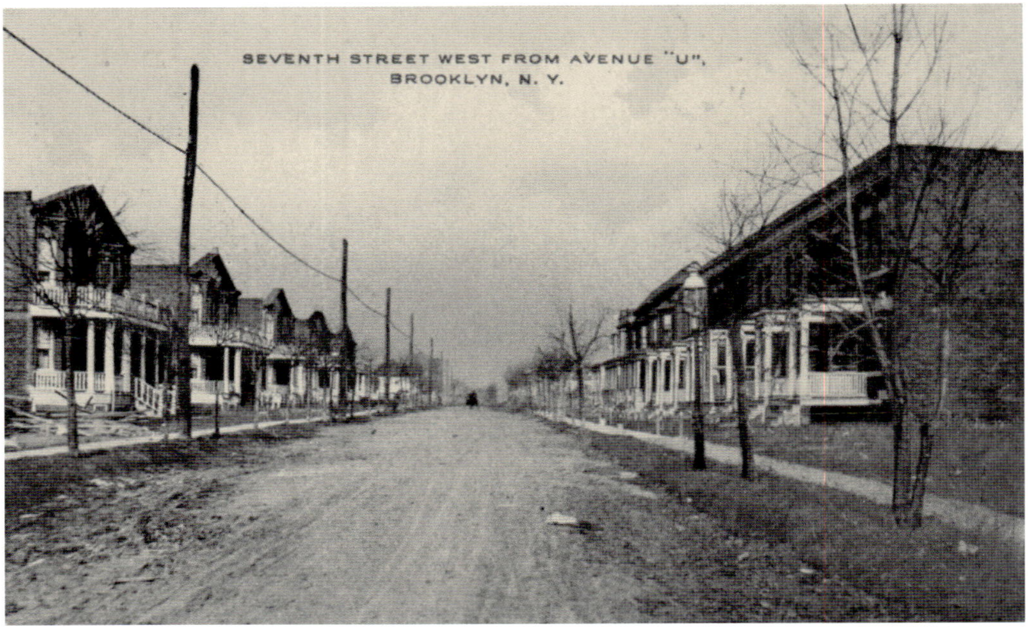

These houses on the 2100 block of East Seventh Street (north of Avenue U) went up around 1909 on one of the many Brooklyn properties held by the colorful real estate speculator Mirabeau Lamar Towns (1850–1932). Towns was an attorney who gained fame as the "poet lawyer" for delivering summations in rhyme. His wife, the educator Christine Towns (about 1859–1939), was equally unconventional: for Christmas 1910 she gave the city's poor children 20,000 toy houses built of cement.

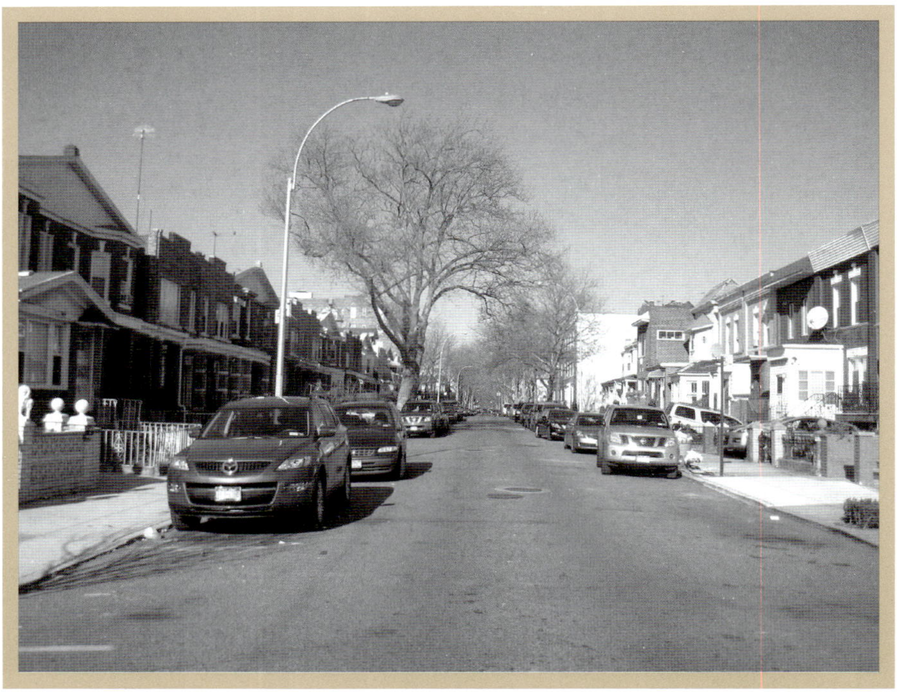

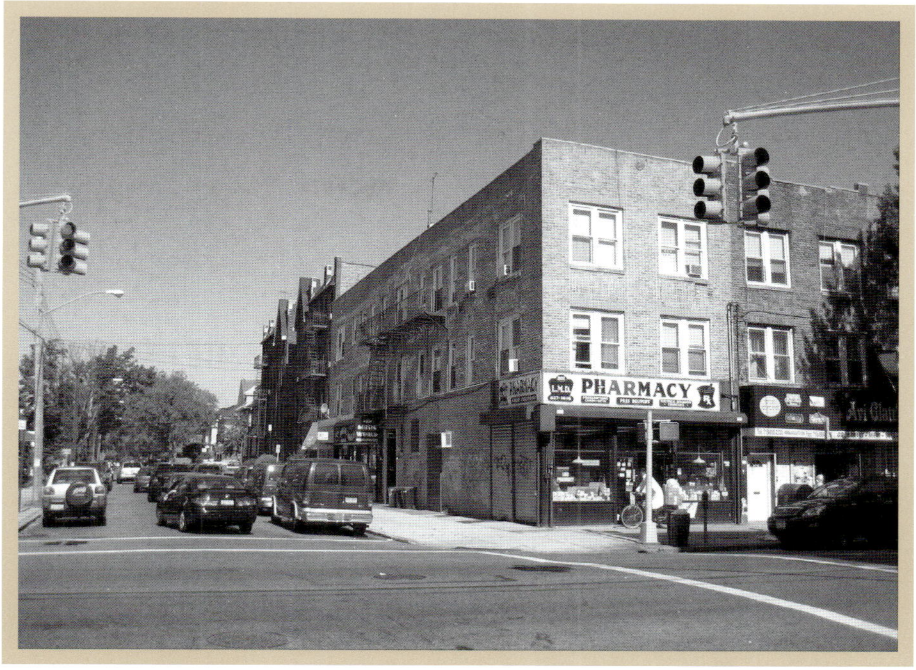

The large stucco house in the old view stood a remarkably short time: erected around 1909 at 803 Avenue U, it was replaced in 1927 by the 10 buildings numbered 801–823 Avenue U. Between 1912 and 1924, it was home to Mary J. McShane (1854–1934), a dealer of antiques and second-hand goods who sold cast-off fashions to ladies who could not otherwise afford couture. Two years before its demolition, the house became the charitable Brooklyn Jewish Home for Convalescents.

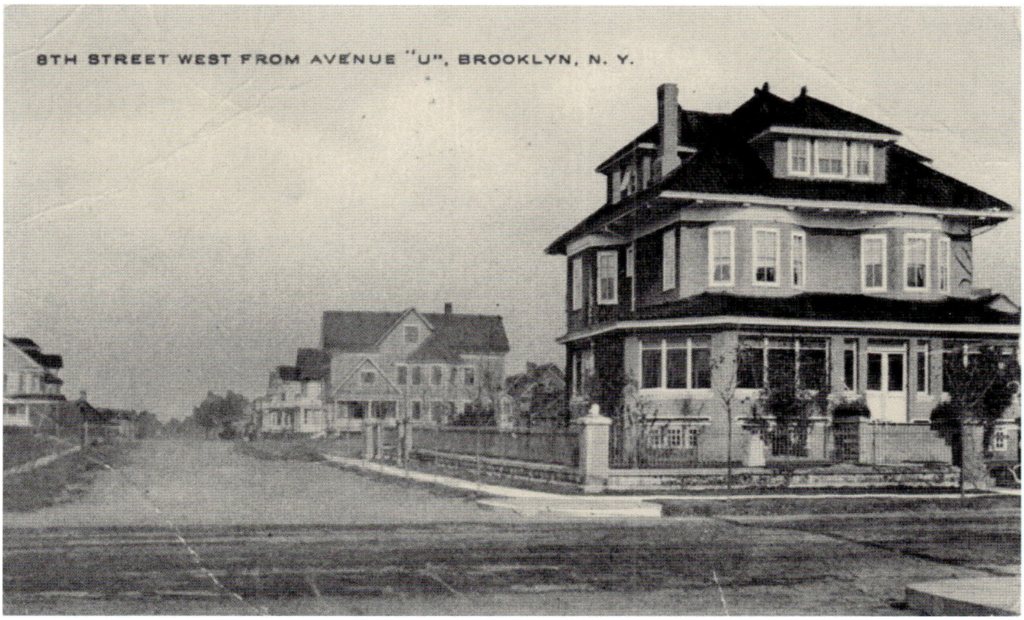

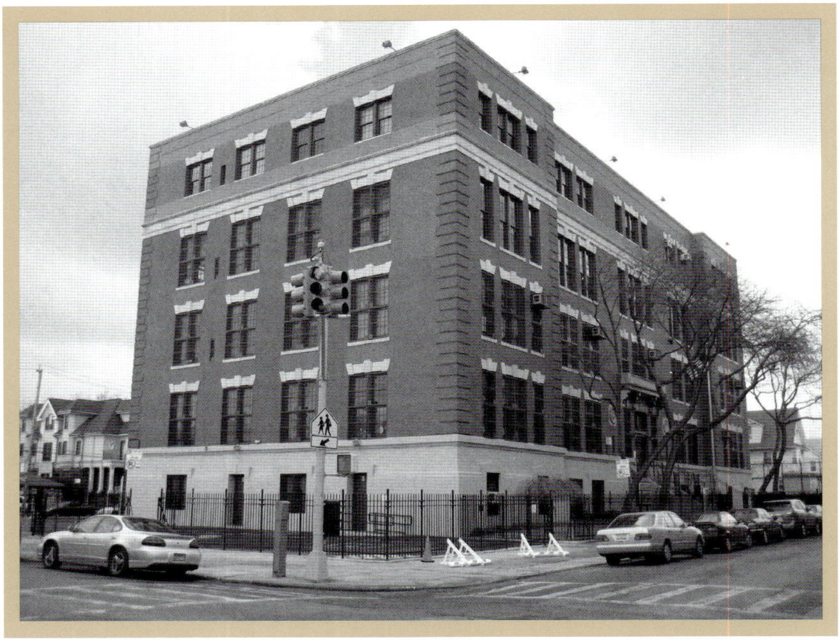

Seen here soon after it opened in 1909, P.S. 153 at 1970 Homecrest Avenue is one of about 400 New York City schools designed by Charles B. J. Snyder (1860–1945), architect for the board of education between 1891 and 1922. The structure follows one of Snyder's standard forms: P.S. 159 at 2781 Pitkin Avenue in East New York is identical. Except for its missing cornice, the building stands largely unchanged. (Courtesy of Michael V. Susi.)

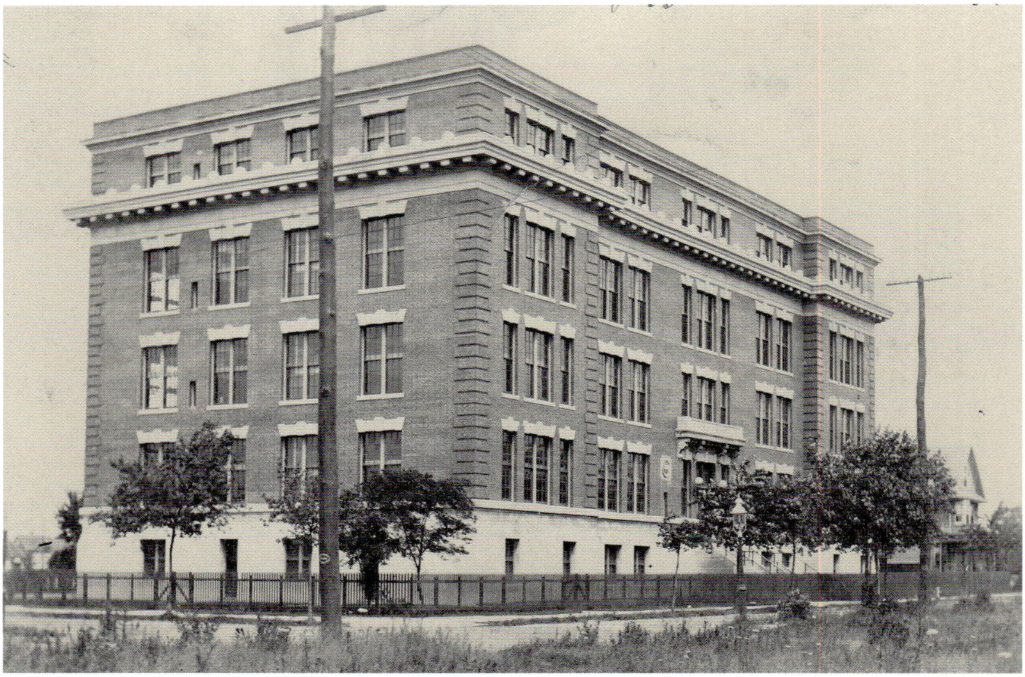

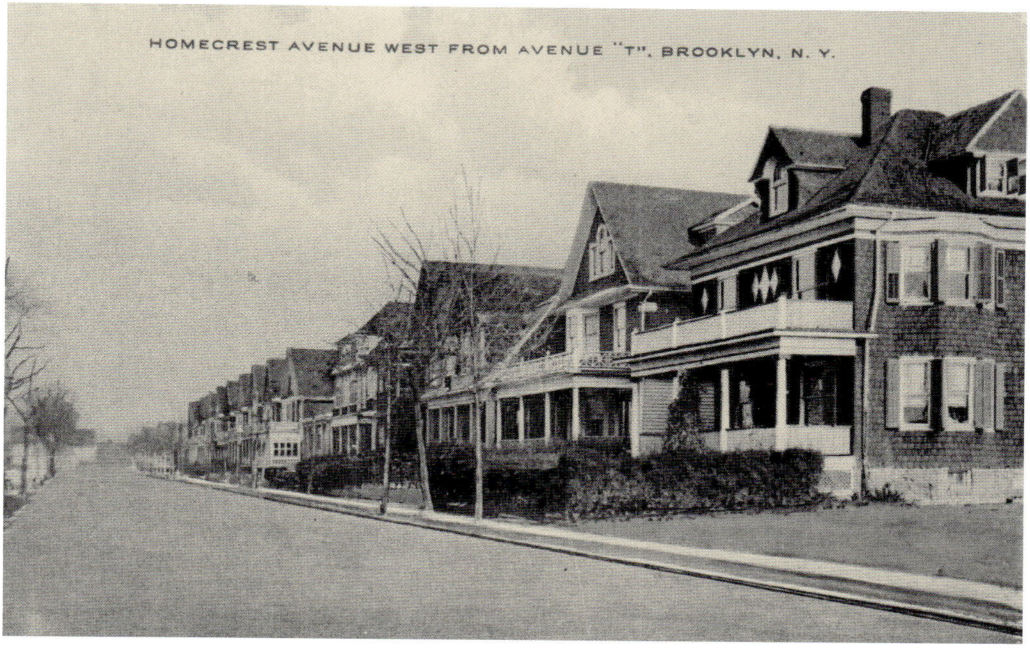

Unlike the forgotten names of most early Gravesend real estate developments, places like Arlington Terrace and Effingham Park, Homecrest has endured since 1898. The neighborhood lies (roughly) between Avenue S, Avenue W, East Eighth Street, and Ocean Avenue. The houses shown here, on the east side of Homecrest Avenue north of Avenue T, went up before 1907. No. 1979 (far right in the old image) was demolished around 1954 to extend the oddly located Beth El Jewish Center of Flatbush.

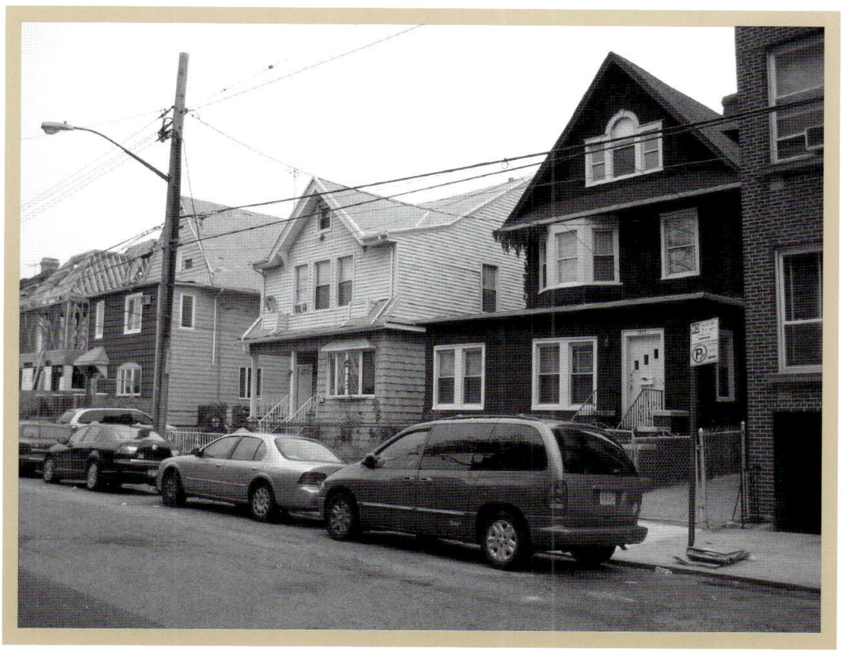

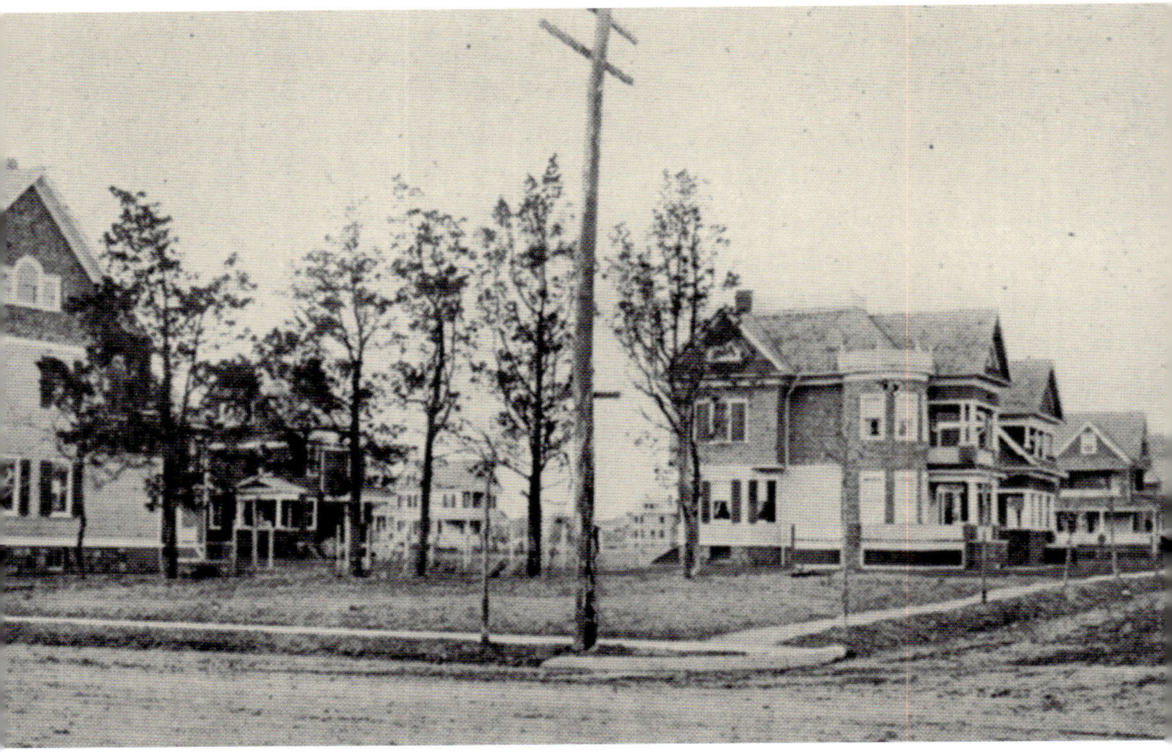

The Harbor and Suburban Building and Savings Association first offered lots at Homecrest in 1898. By 1903, roads, gas mains, and sewers were in place, electric lights lit the avenues, and 2,000 silver maples had been planted. The neighborhood took shape that year as 100 houses neared completion. Some have been demolished and many altered beyond recognition, but the house right of center in the 1908 view—No. 2068 East Fourteenth Street, north of Avenue U—retains its basic shape.

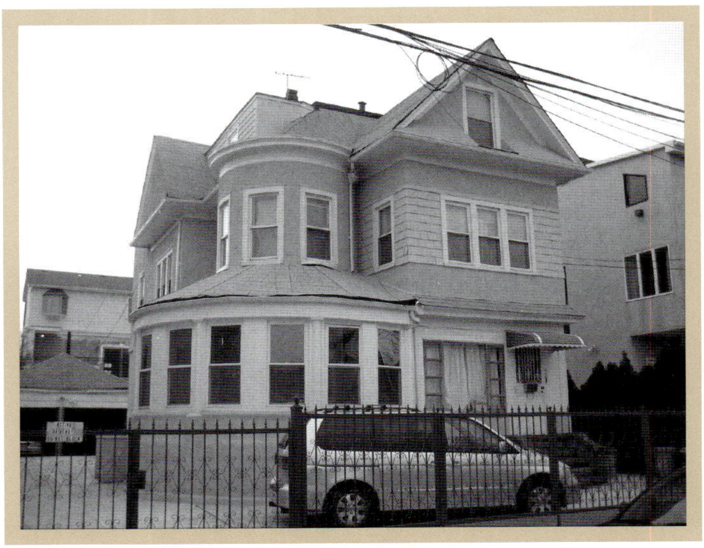

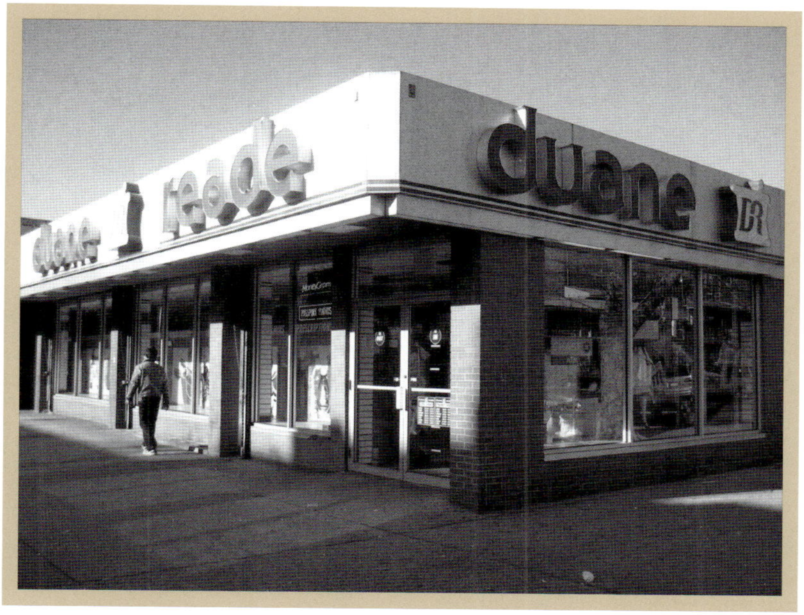

The grandest building in Homecrest was the Italian Renaissance Revival–style police station at the northwest corner of Avenue U and East Fifteenth Street. Erected in 1904, it housed a succession of shifting precinct headquarters: the 168th, the 72nd, and ultimately, the 61st. The 61st Precinct left the building in 1977 for a banal, modern structure at 2575 Coney Island Avenue. The abandoned station was demolished after 1979; its site now lies near the center of a bustling Asian American community.

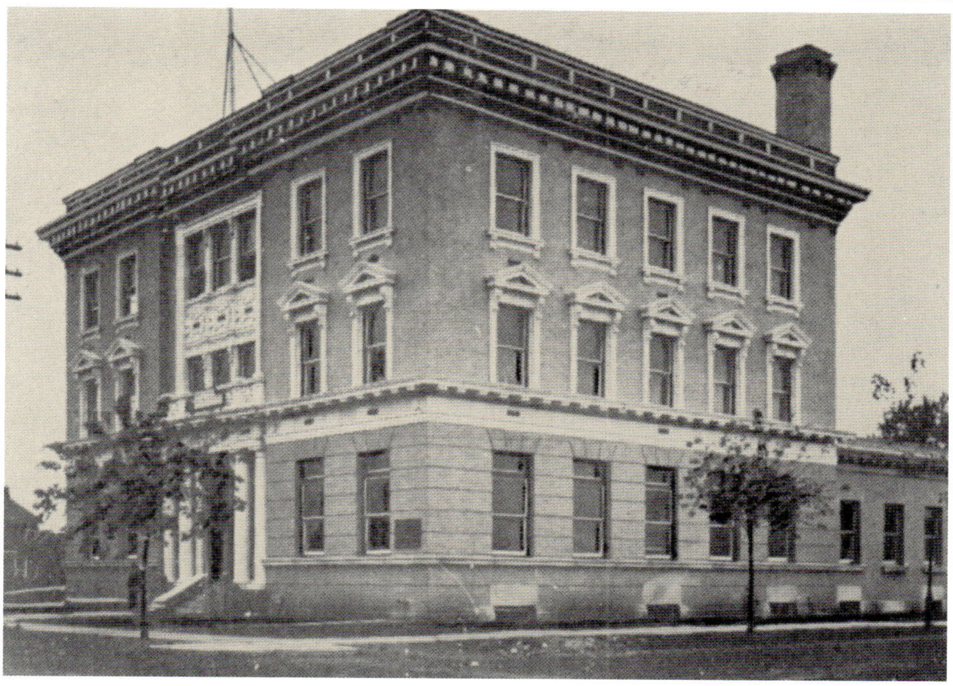

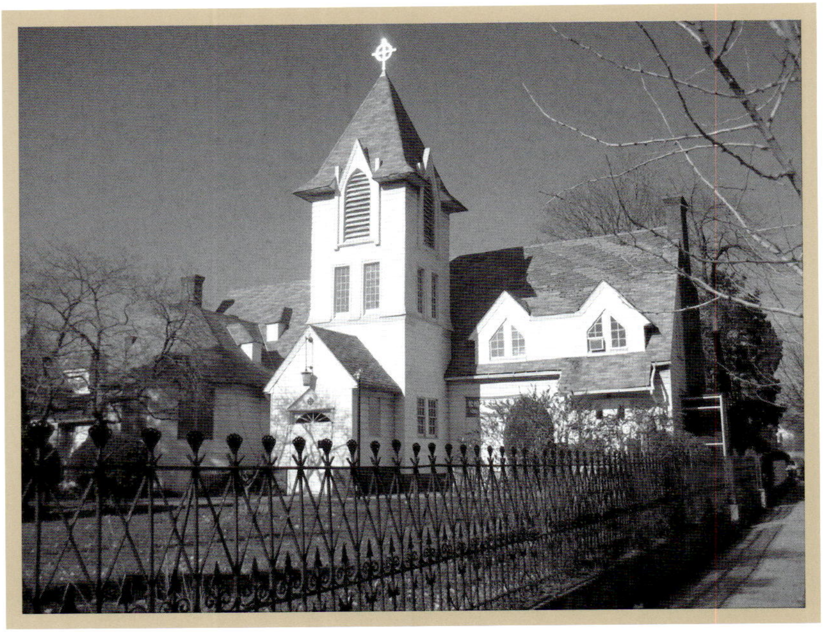

Set back on an expansive lawn at 1413 Avenue T, the Homecrest Presbyterian Church was dedicated on Easter Sunday, 1901. The early image shows the building before it was extended eastward in 1922. The fence enclosing the grounds is much older than the church: photographs confirm it was salvaged from the front yards of London Terrace, a row of Greek Revival–style houses that stood on West Twenty-third Street in Chelsea, Manhattan, from 1845 until 1929. (Courtesy of Michael V. Susi.)

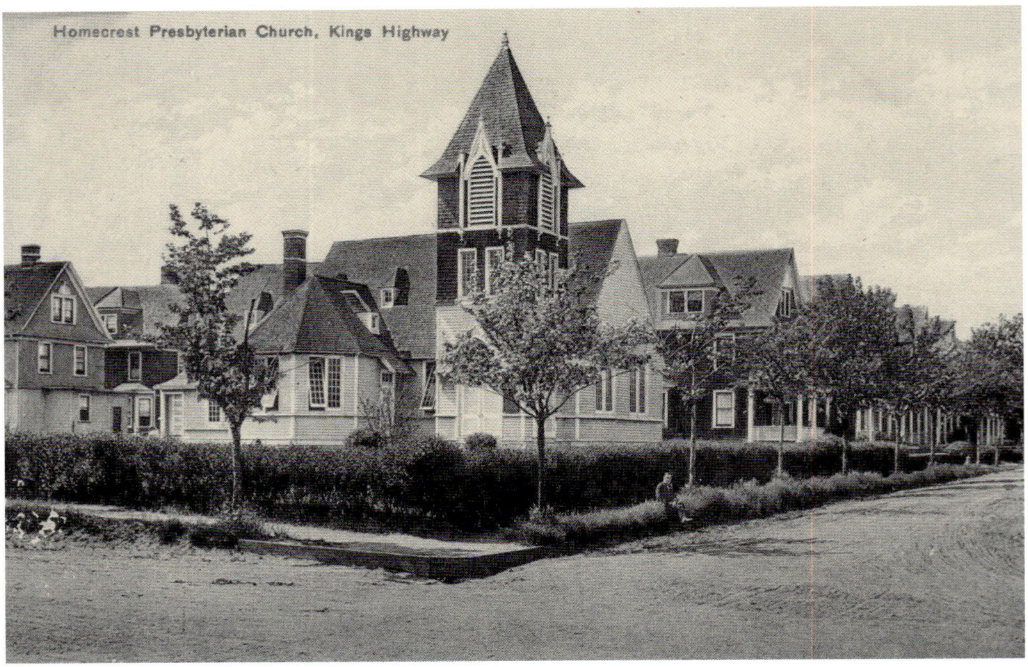

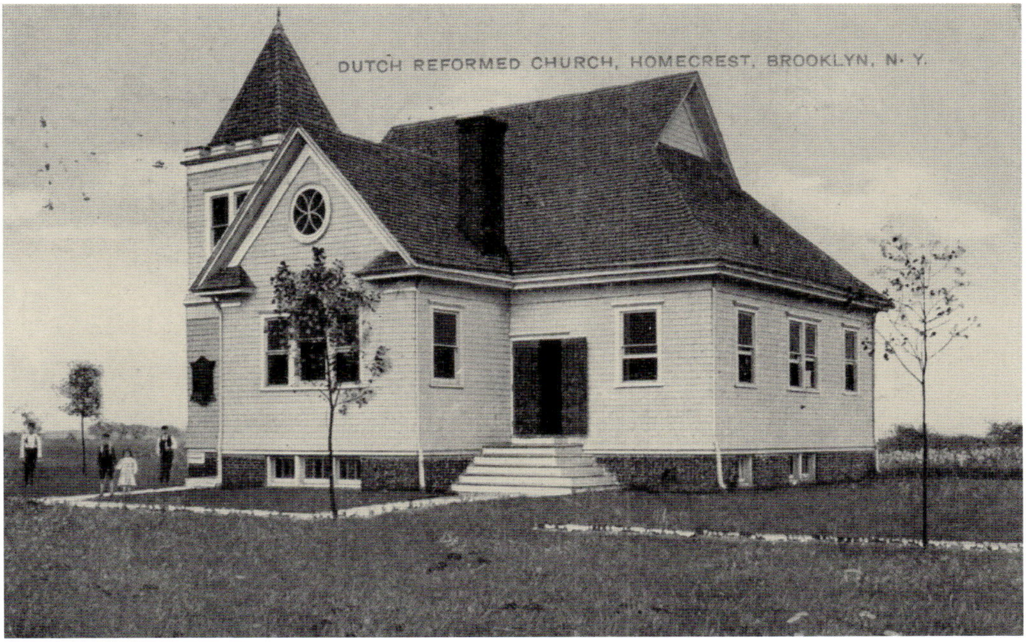

A "neck" of land extends into water. Gravesend Neck juts between Sheepshead Bay and Gerritsen's Creek. To serve its members in this distant corner of town, the Reformed Dutch Church built a Gravesend Neck chapel in 1868. Its replacement and final home, dedicated in 1907 at the southeast corner of Avenue T and East Twenty-first Street, mimics the shape of the parent church on page 38. No longer used for its intended function, the chapel has recently undergone extensive alteration.

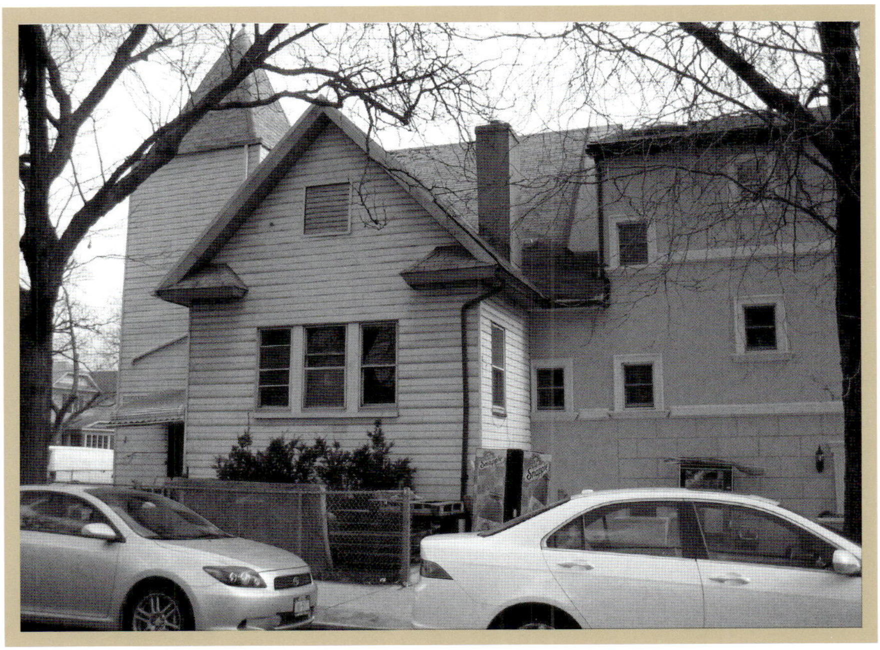

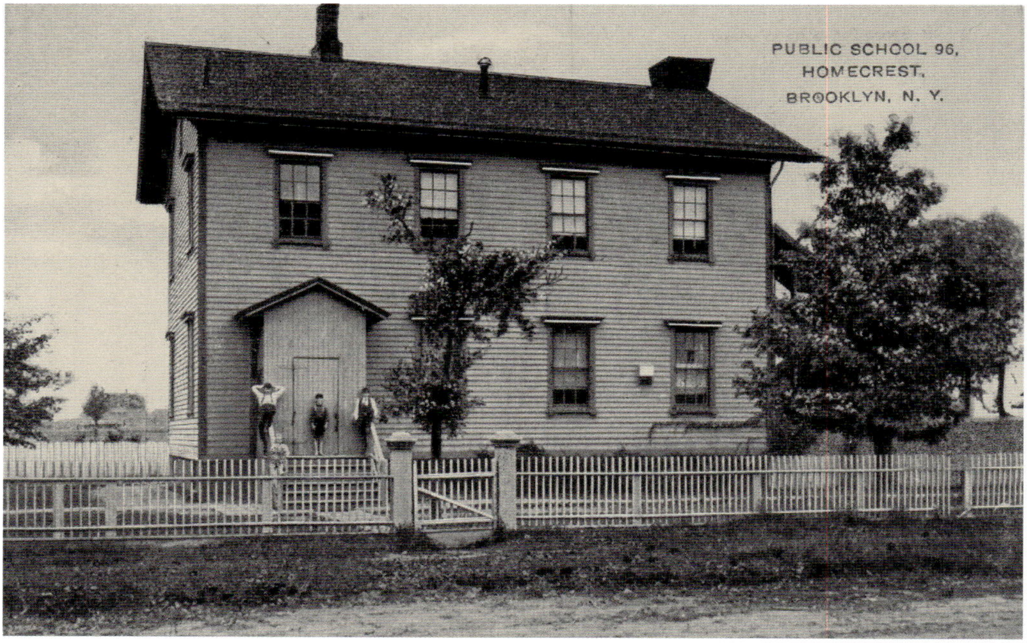

The four-room wooden schoolhouse near the northeast corner of Ocean Avenue and Avenue U was built in 1879. Originally Gravesend's District No. 2 school, it was renumbered P.S. 96 when Brooklyn annexed the town in 1894. Nicknamed the "chicken coop" for the barnyard structure it resembled, it was likely as primitive inside as another early Gravesend school where "cold air blew up out of the wide cracks of the plank floor." It was demolished around 1925.

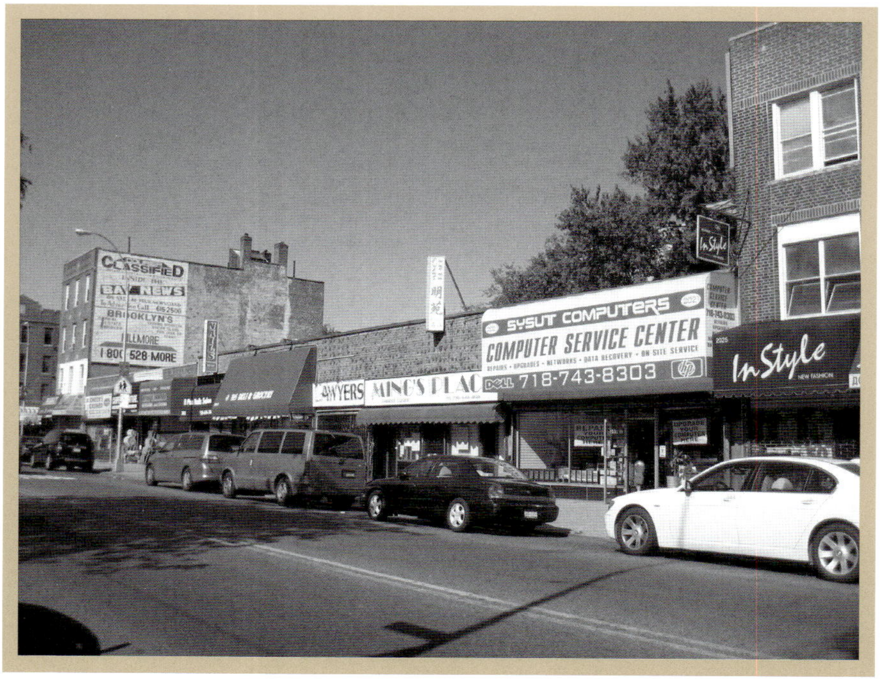

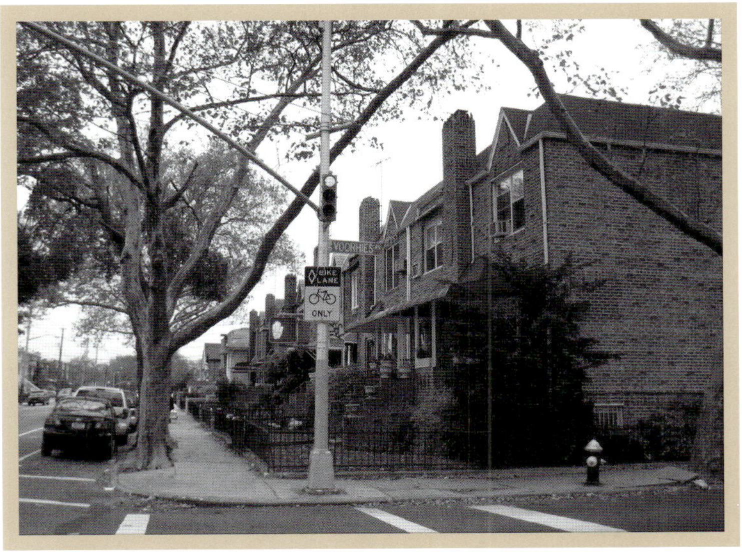

John Y. McKane (1841–1899), Gravesend's corrupt town supervisor (in 1894, he was sentenced to six years hard labor for election fraud) was a carpenter by trade. Between 1866 and 1884, he built two-thirds of the structures in Gravesend. His own home, the Italianate-style villa in the 1909 photograph, stood until 1931 at the northeast corner of Voorhies and Bedford Avenues in Sheepshead Bay. The brick houses currently on the site at 4685–4705 Bedford Avenue were completed in 1939.

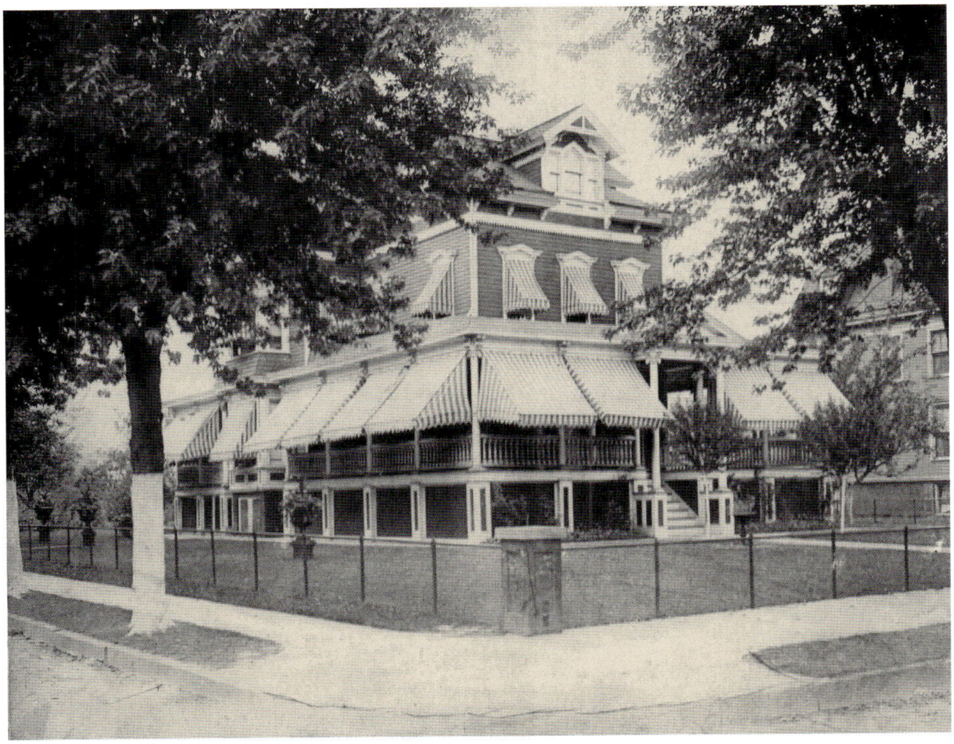

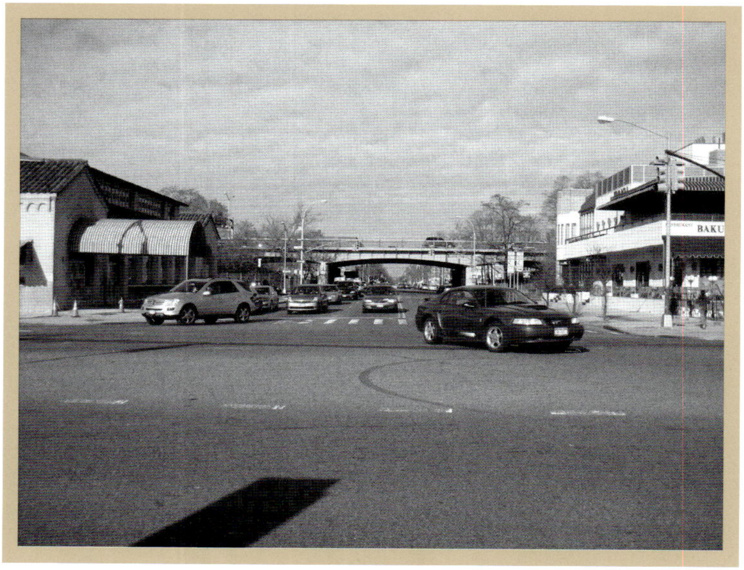

In contrast to the $1 million spent on elaborate Ocean Parkway, it cost just $15,000 to build Ocean Avenue between Flatbush Avenue and Sheepshead Bay in 1876. The street stops at Emmons Avenue, then continues across the water for three blocks in Manhattan Beach. The 2,800-seat F.W.I.L. Lundy Brothers Restaurant opened in 1934 at the northwest corner of Ocean and Emmons Avenues (at left in the current photograph). It closed in 1979, but has since had several reincarnations.

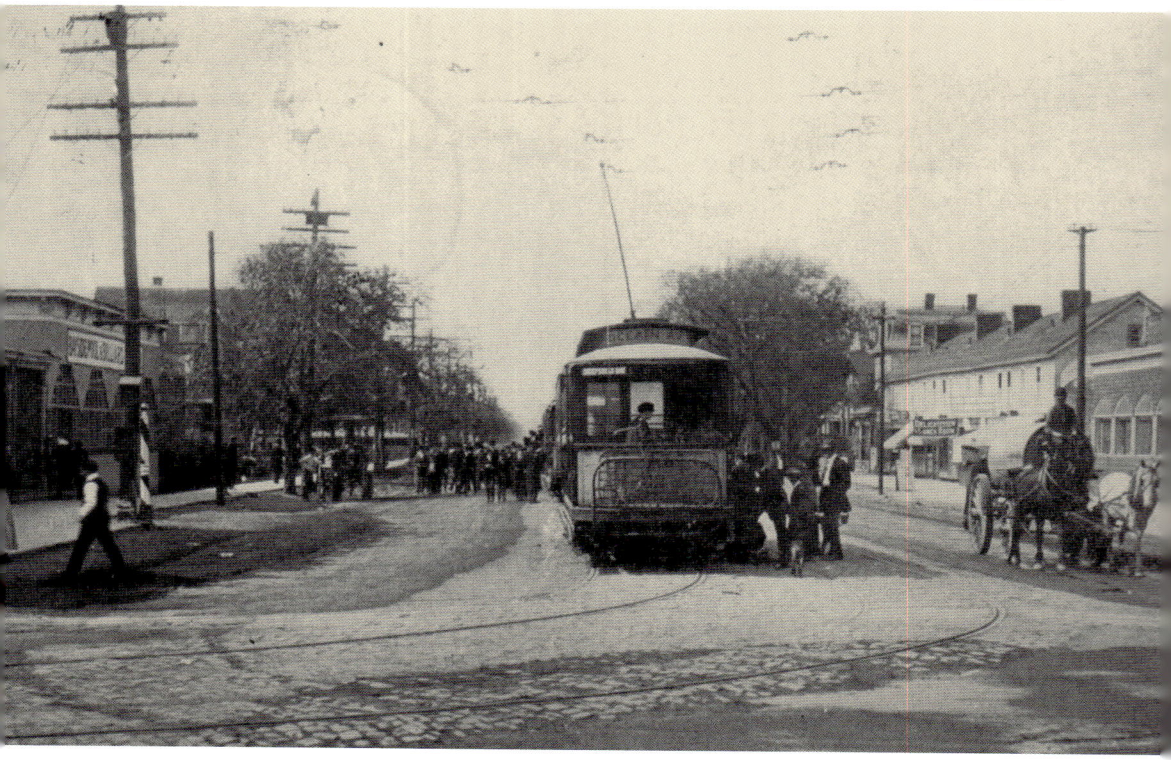

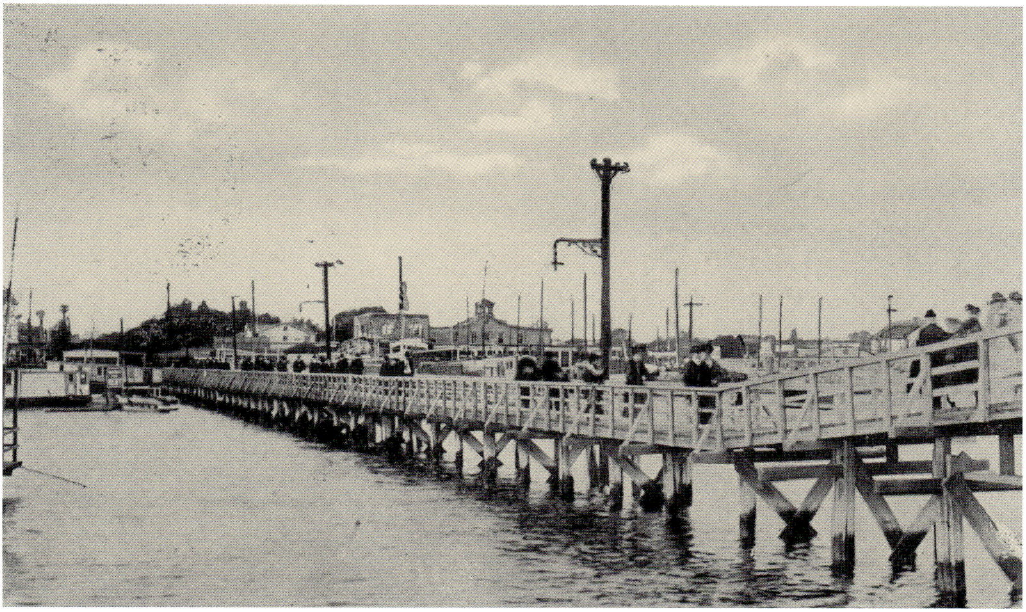

Despite its name, the Ocean Avenue Bridge over Sheepshead Bay does not connect the interrupted segments of that roadway. Rather, the 470-foot pedestrian span links East Nineteenth Street to Shore Boulevard in Manhattan Beach. The first bridge across this spot opened in 1880; it was rebuilt several times, most recently in 1917. A portion of the current structure collapsed when the seawall crumbled in 2005. A pontoon bridge provided temporary access while the rickety walkway was restored.

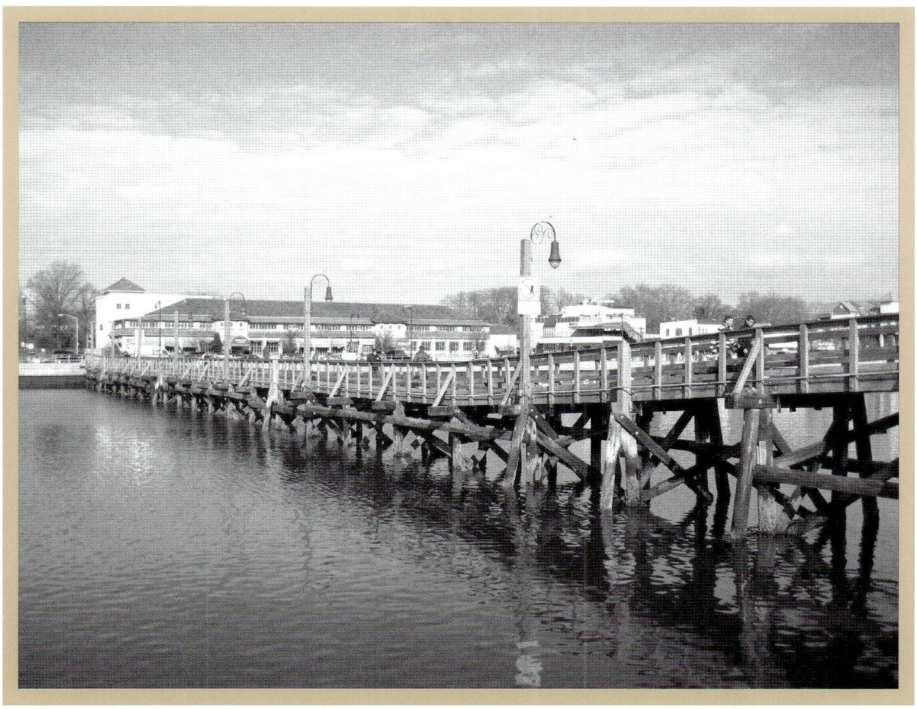

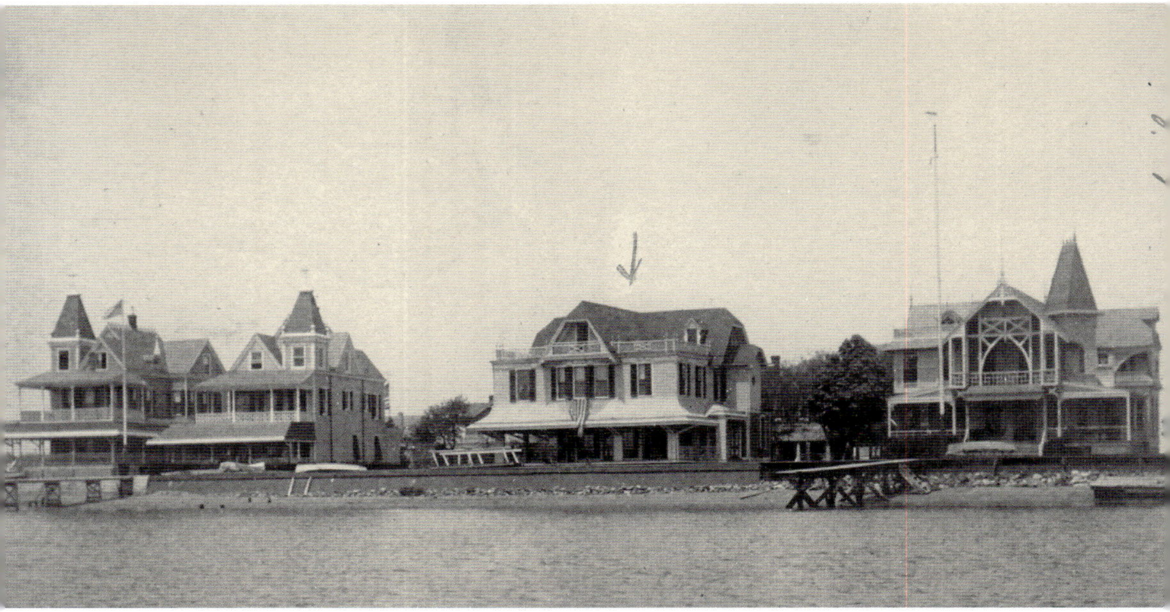

By the last quarter of the 19th century, Gravesend's quiet seaside village of Sheepshead Bay (named for the sheepshead, a fish once common in its waters) attracted wealthy residents. They built lavish summer "cottages" like those in the pre-1907 photograph. Part of so-called Millionaires' Row, these four houses lined the shore between East Twenty-eighth and Twenty-ninth Streets. Just one survives: 2806 Emmons Avenue (at far left), now home to the Varuna Boat Club (organized elsewhere in 1875).

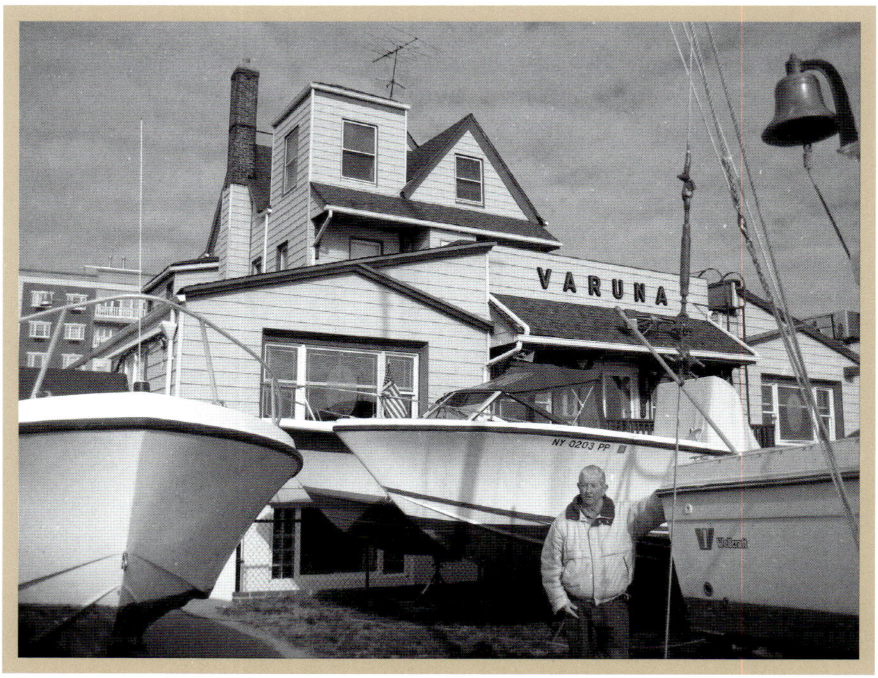

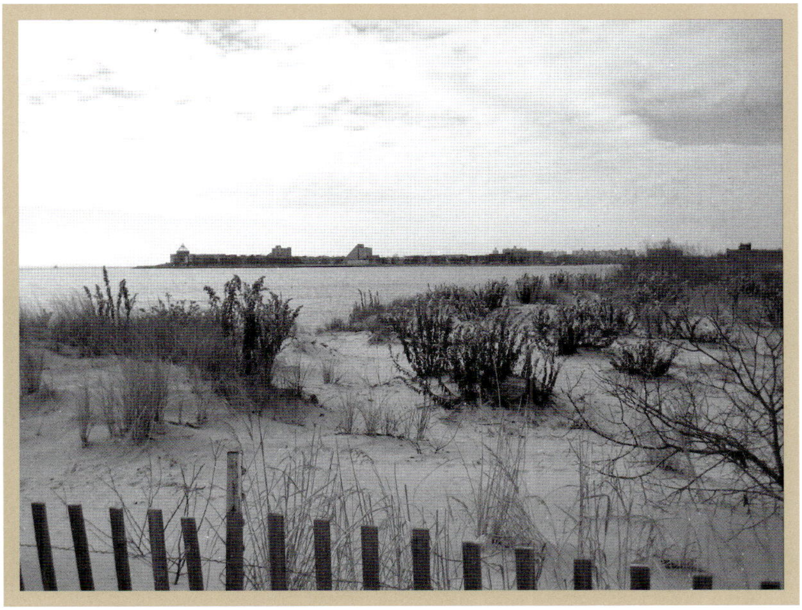

A far more modest settlement than Millionaires' Row evolved on Plumb Beach, an island east of Sheepshead Bay. (Spelled both with and without a final "b," the island's name came from the plums that grew wild among the dunes.) The community's simple tents, shown here in 1923, were accessible only by rowboat or at low tide. Construction of the Belt Parkway (opened in 1940) joined Plumb Beach to mainland Brooklyn, but forced its residents to find other homes.

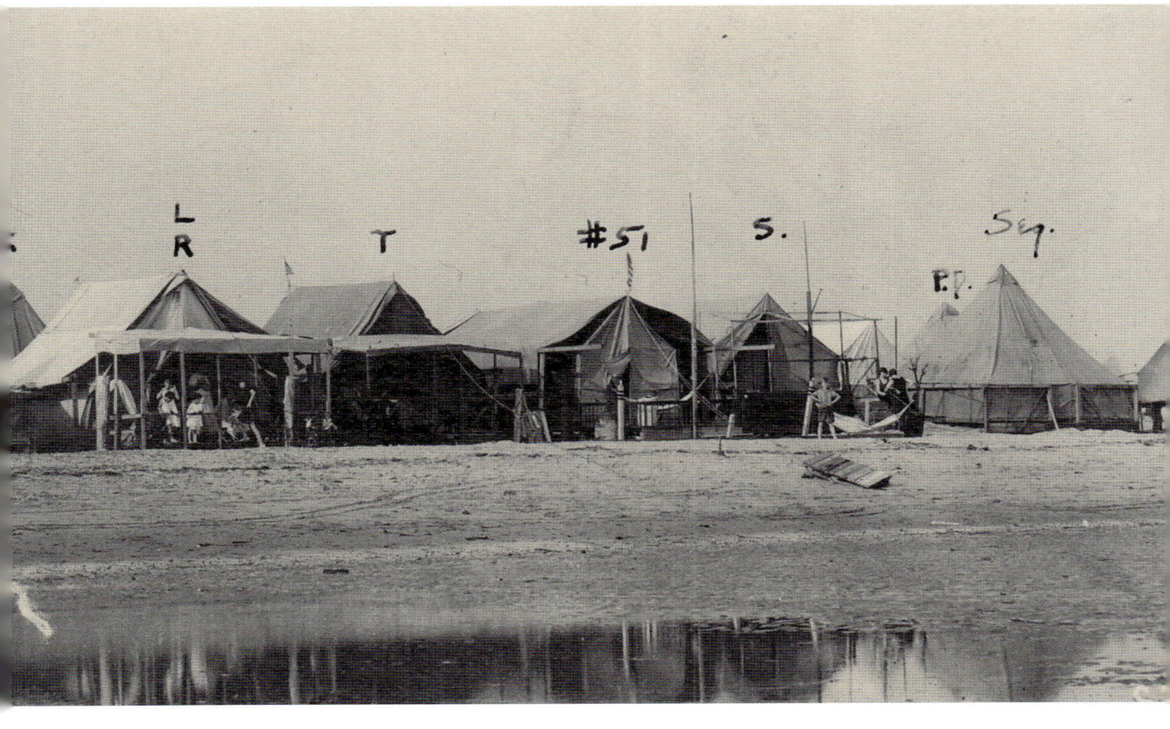

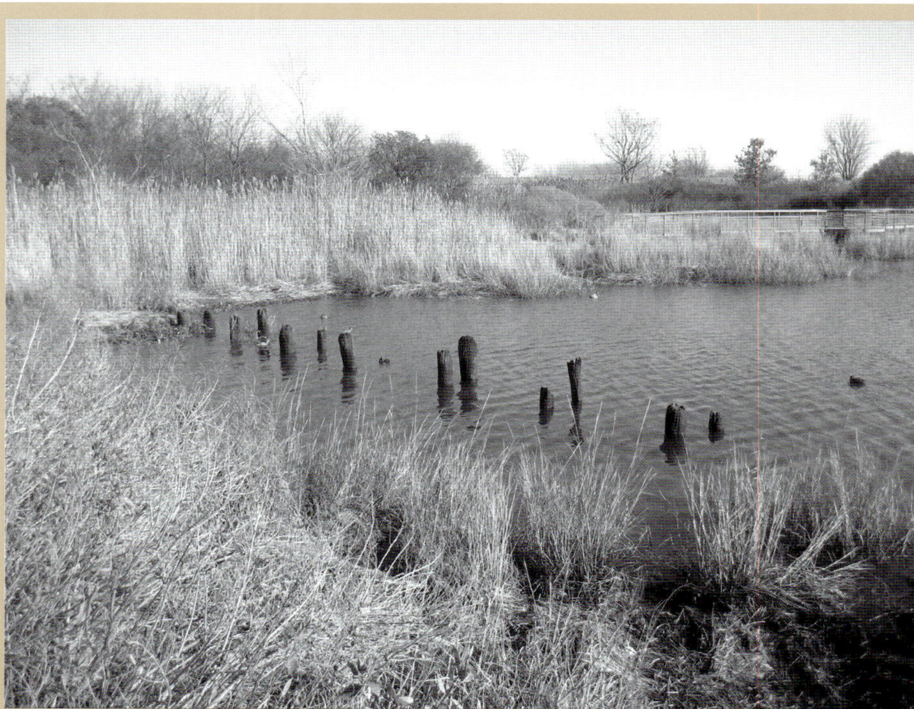

The Dutch on southwestern Long Island did not generally build windmills to grind grain. Instead they dammed tidal inlets to turn the wheels of water-powered gristmills. The Gerritsen family operated a tide mill on the Gravesend side of the Strome Kill (or Gerritsen's Creek, in Marine Park), opposite Flatlands, from the 17th century until the 1890s. Their last mill building (seen here) burned in 1935, but the pilings from its dam across the creek remain visible at low tide.

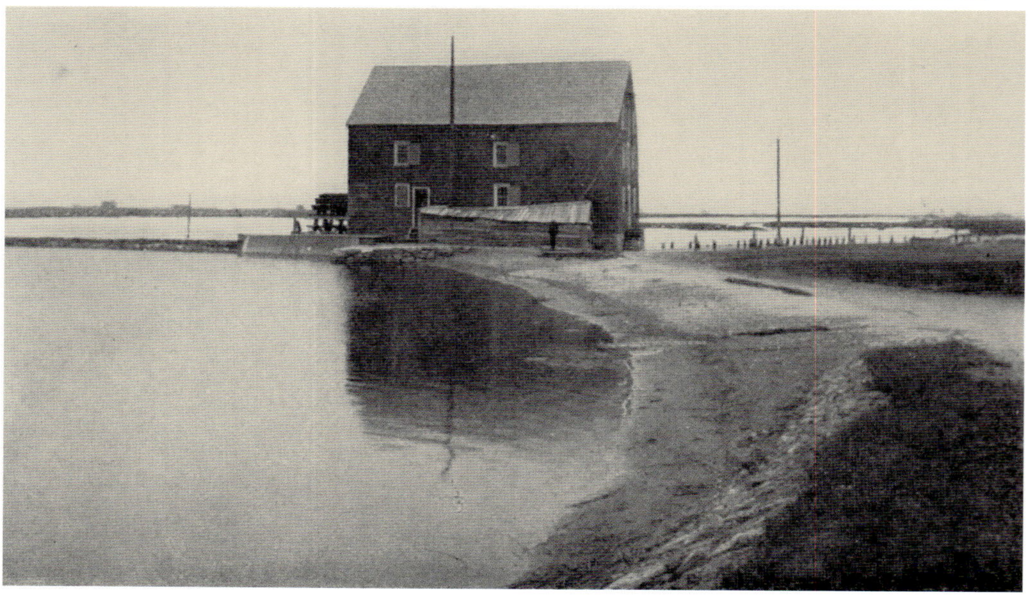

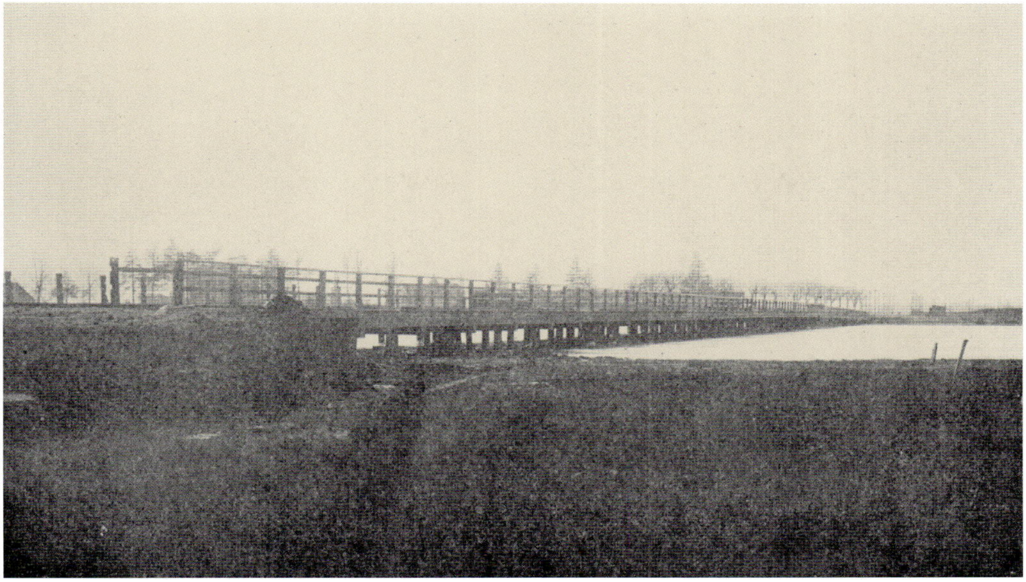

Until the early 20th century, Gerritsen's Creek reached a mile farther inland than it does today. Before 1902, crossing was by boat or detour to Kings Highway. That year a 756-foot trestle was built to carry Avenue U over the marshes, bridging the former towns of Flatlands and Gravesend. Dredging, begun in 1931, truncated the creek, put the roadway on landfill, and created Marine Park's ball fields between Avenue U and Fillmore Avenue. (Courtesy of the New-York Historical Society.)

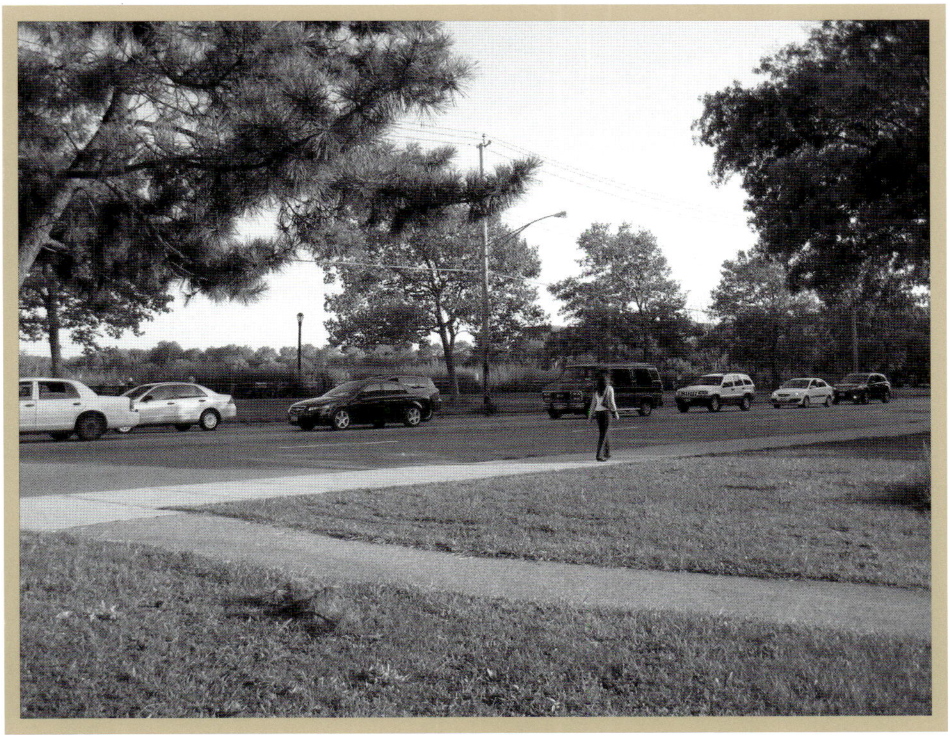

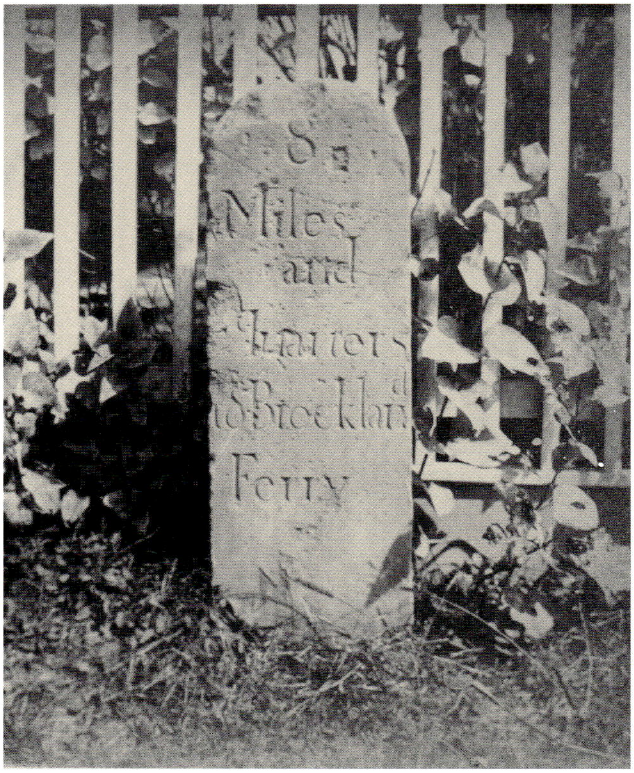

This milestone stood beside the farmhouse of Judge Nicholas Stillwell (1808–1885) at the now-obliterated intersection of Gravesend Neck Road and Ryder's Lane (roughly 20 feet north of Avenue U between Haring and Brown Streets). Its archaic inscription—"8 Miles and [3] Quarters to Brockland Ferry"—told the distance to Brooklyn Ferry on the East River. Around 1930, the stone was moved to a Brown Street backyard and soon disappeared. See page 62 for a surviving Gravesend milestone.

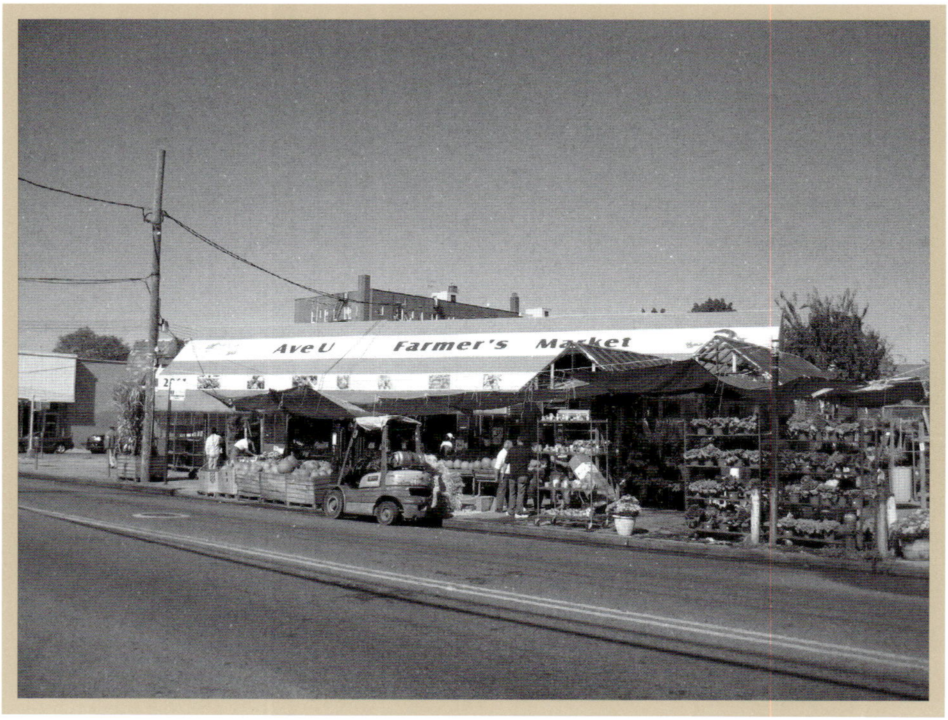

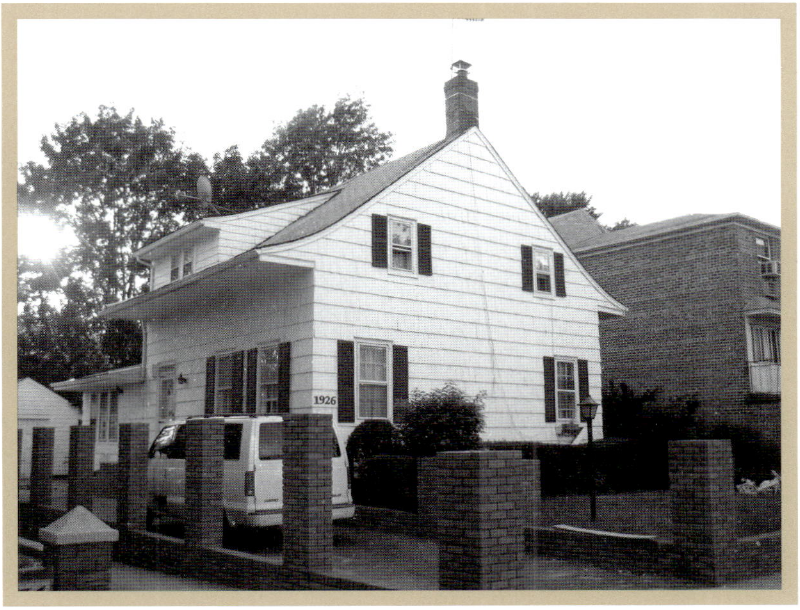

Elias Hubbard Ryder (1796–1875) built this house in the traditional Dutch style in 1834. Originally positioned on Ryder's Lane (laid out about 1831 between Kings Highway and Gravesend Neck Road), the house stood in the projected roadbed of East Twenty-ninth Street just south of Avenue S. When that street was cut through around 1930, the house was moved one block west to 1926 East Twenty-eighth Street, where it stands today with slight alterations. It gained landmark status in 1976.

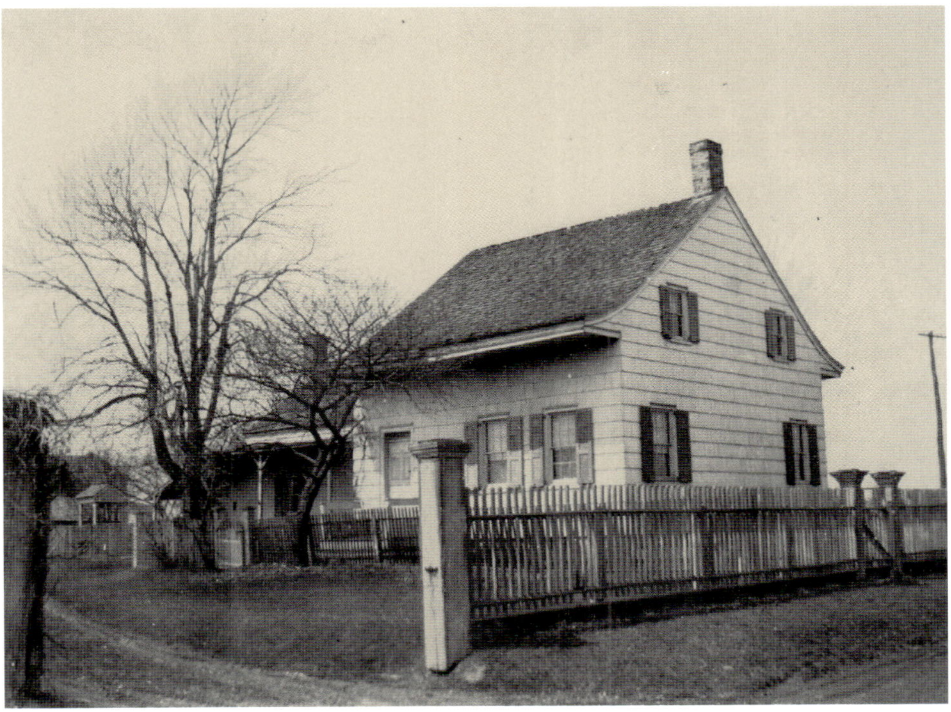

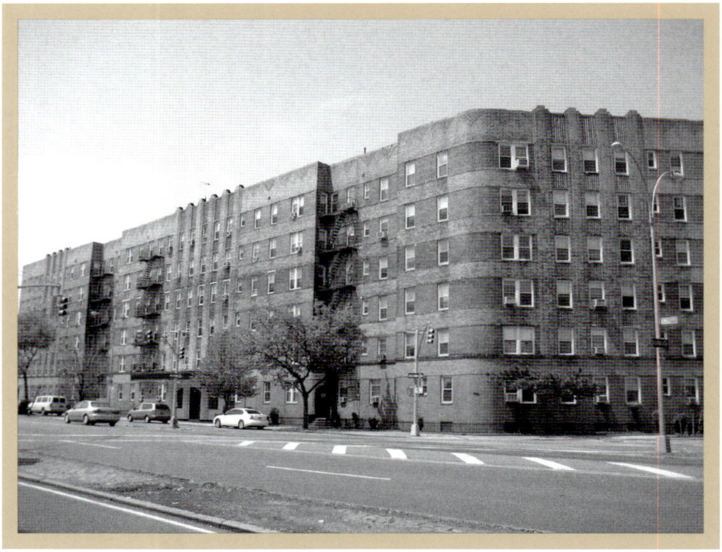

Judge Isaac Terhune (1762–1835) built this elegant Georgian-style residence in 1812 on the edge of South Greenfield, a village in northern Gravesend. Affluent lawyer Benjamin G. Hitchings (1813–1893) bought the house and adjacent 70 acres in 1853. In 1897, his heirs sold the property to real estate developers, who subdivided it into Hitchings Homestead, but the house survived until 1928. The 94-family art deco–style apartment building at 2301 Kings Highway has occupied its site since 1935.

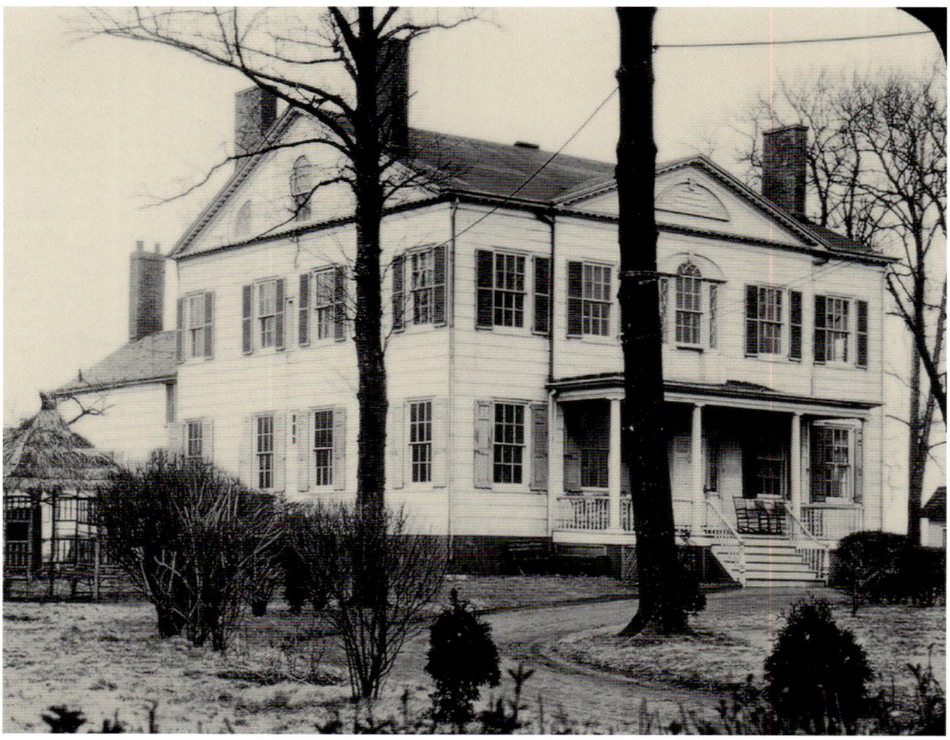

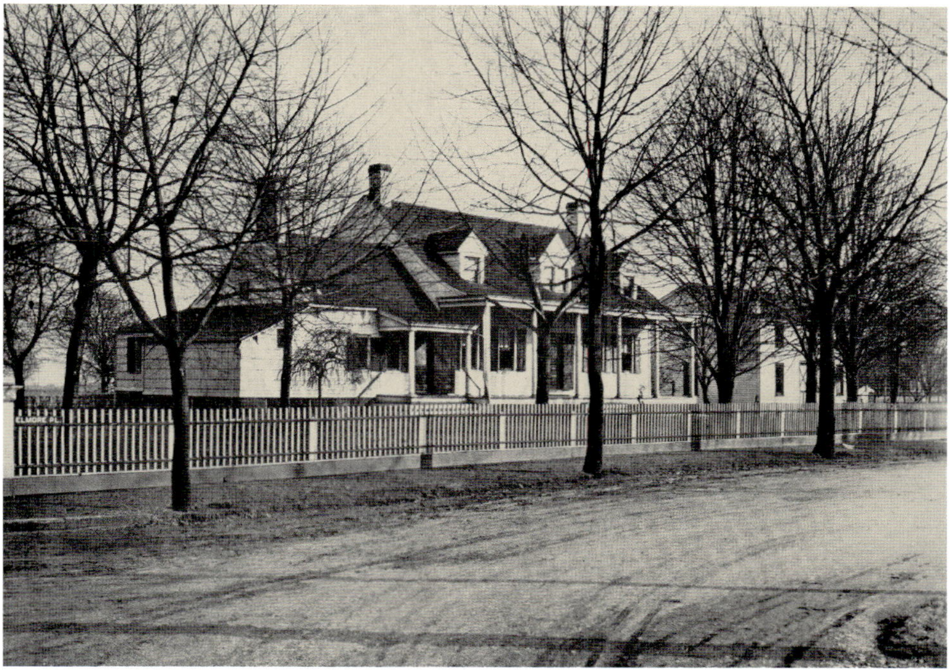

Set behind a long picket fence, the landmarked Wyckoff-Bennett Homestead is considered the most beautiful of Brooklyn's Dutch farmhouses. Built before 1766 by Hendrick Wyckoff, it quartered Hessian officers during the Revolution. Cornelius Bennett bought the property in 1835. About 1900, his son, William, sold the surrounding 100 acres, shifted the house to 1669 East Twenty-second Street, and added its dormers, porch, and graceful columns. William's granddaughter, the poet-historian Gertrude Ryder Bennett (1901–1982), drew inspiration from her lifelong home.

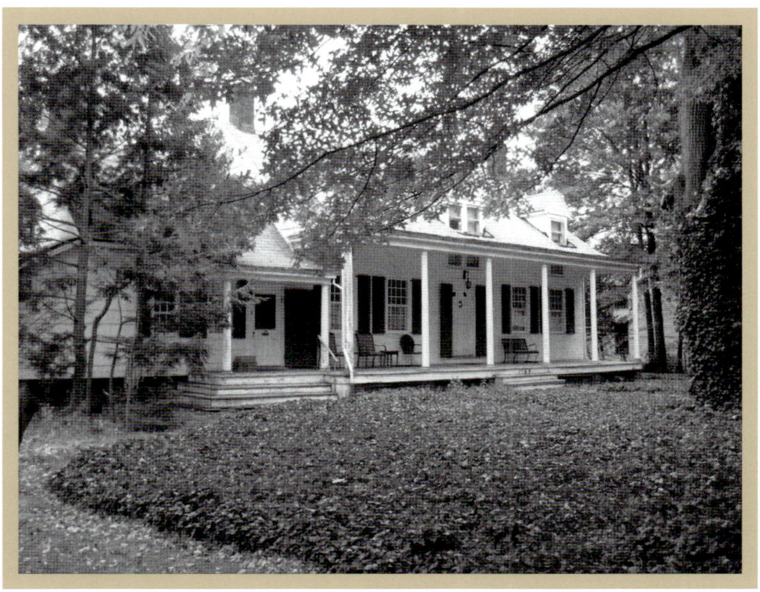

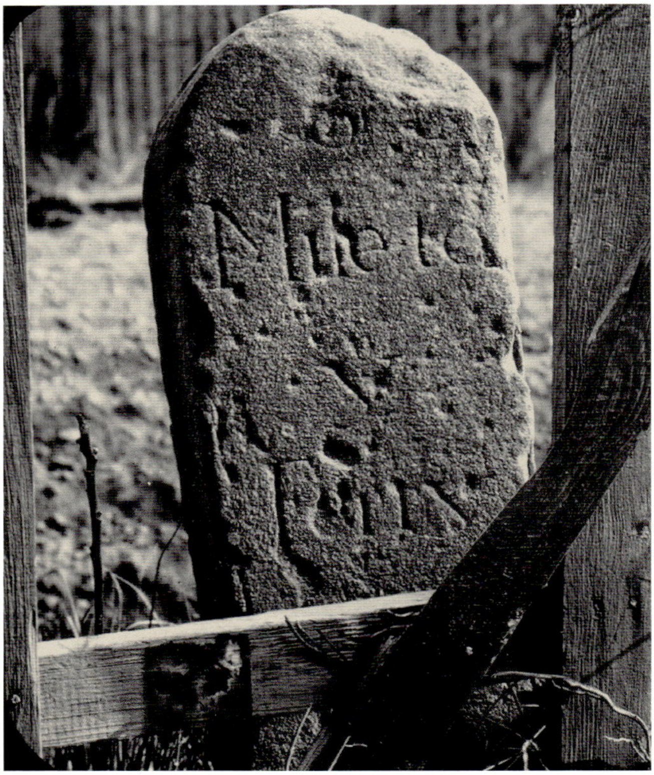

The battered inscription on this 18th-century milestone—"6 Mile[s] to Ye Ferry"—told travelers the distance to Denyse's Wharf on Gravesend Bay opposite Staten Island (near the Brooklyn tower of the Verrazano-Narrows Bridge). The stone stood approximately at 1916 Kings Highway, on the farm of Elias Ryder Bennett (1847–1927), who gave it to the Kings County Historical Society in 1921. When that organization dissolved in 1940, the stone was transferred to the Long Island (now Brooklyn) Historical Society.

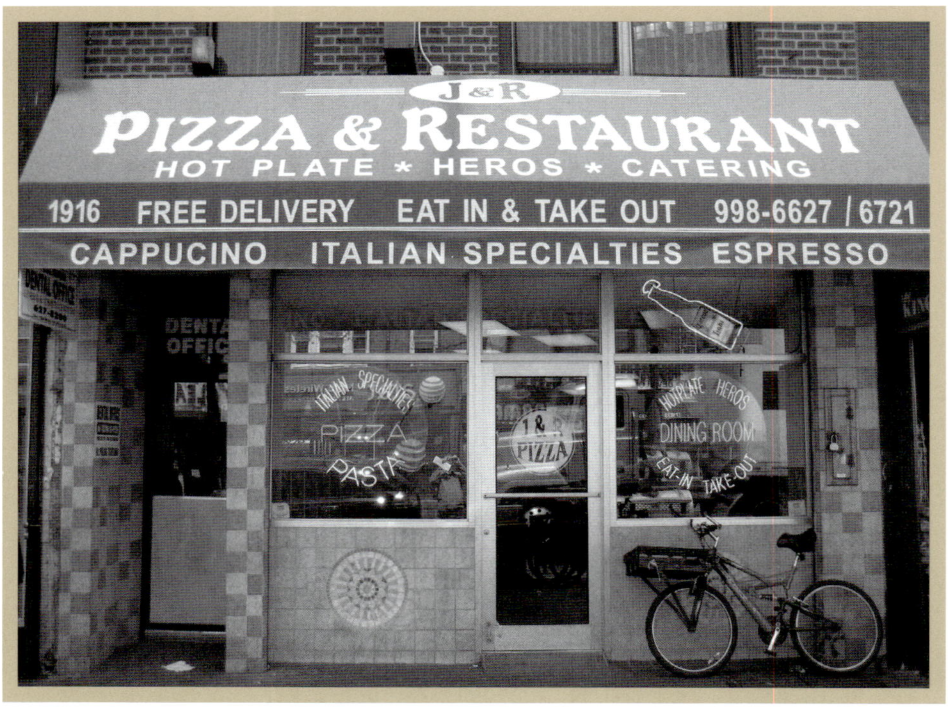

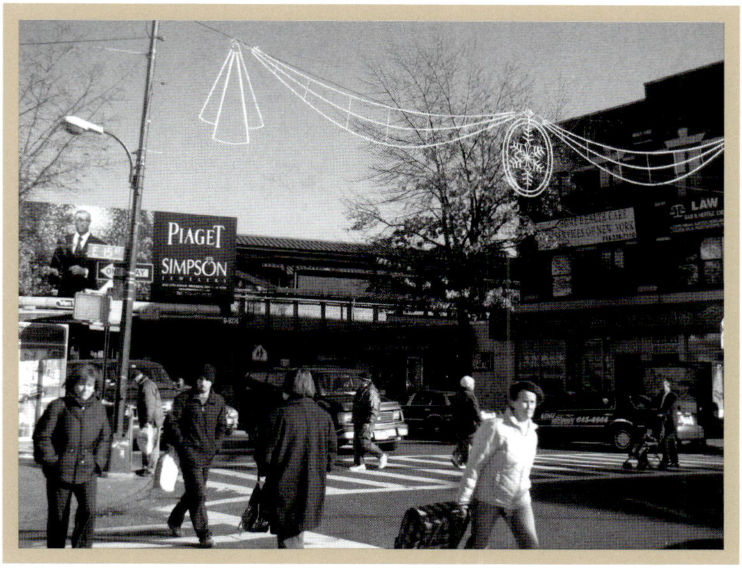

The Brooklyn, Flatbush, and Coney Island Railroad, better known as the Brighton Line, opened in 1878 between Atlantic Avenue and the Brighton Beach Hotel, its seaside terminus. The Brighton Line was electrified in 1899, and in 1905–1908 the tracks south of Foster Avenue were set on an embankment to eliminate grade crossings in rapidly developing Gravesend. The Kings Highway station (seen here), one of the line's busiest, is serviced today by B (express) and Q (local) trains.

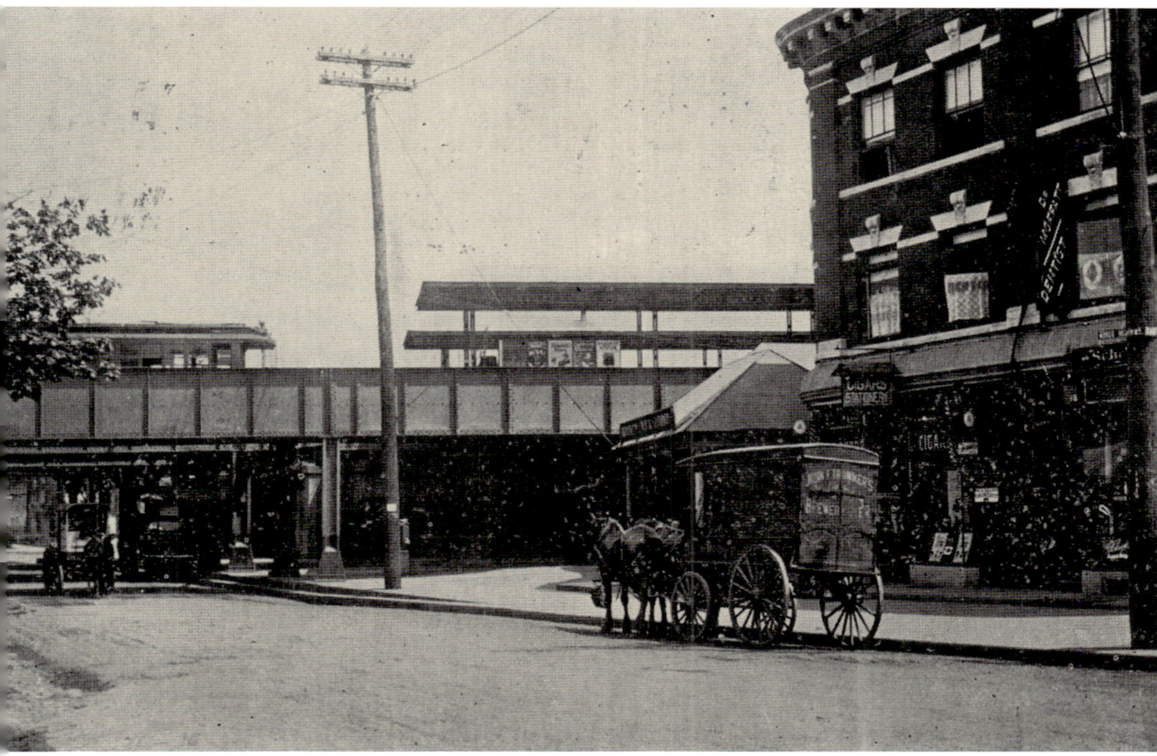

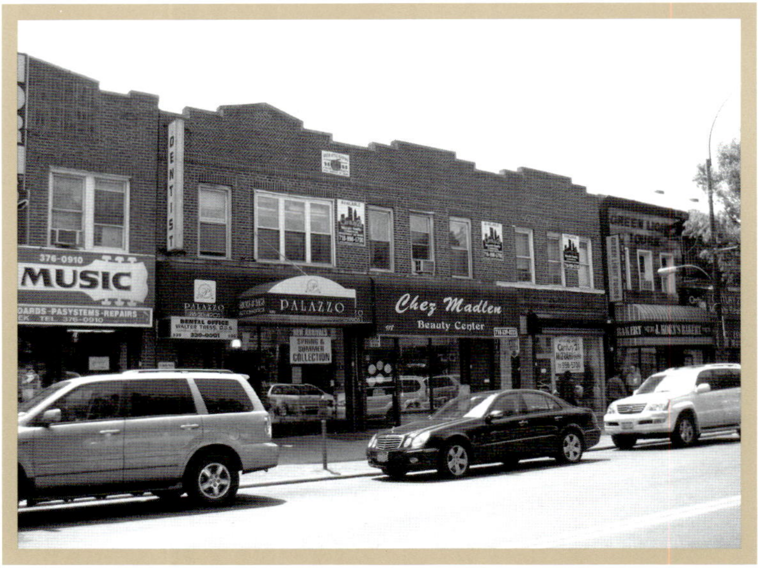

The sprawling Manhattan department store founded by Edward Ridley (1816–1883) once employed 1,700—a workforce larger than the 1865 population of Gravesend (1,627). Ridley lived in Gravesend, in the French Second Empire–style mansion he built about 1866 near 914–920 Kings Highway, shown here in 1884. His daughter, Clara (Ridley) Gerken (1867–1948), later trained horses on the surrounding 23 acres, which she dubbed Gerkendale Farm. She sold her prize-winning stock in 1907. Her father's house was demolished around 1924.

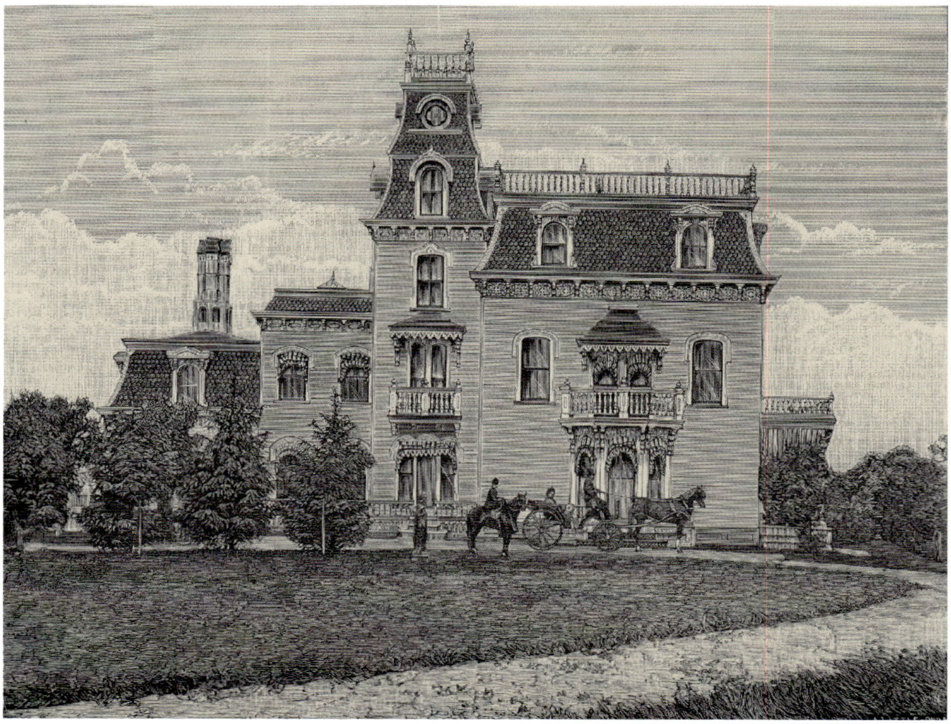

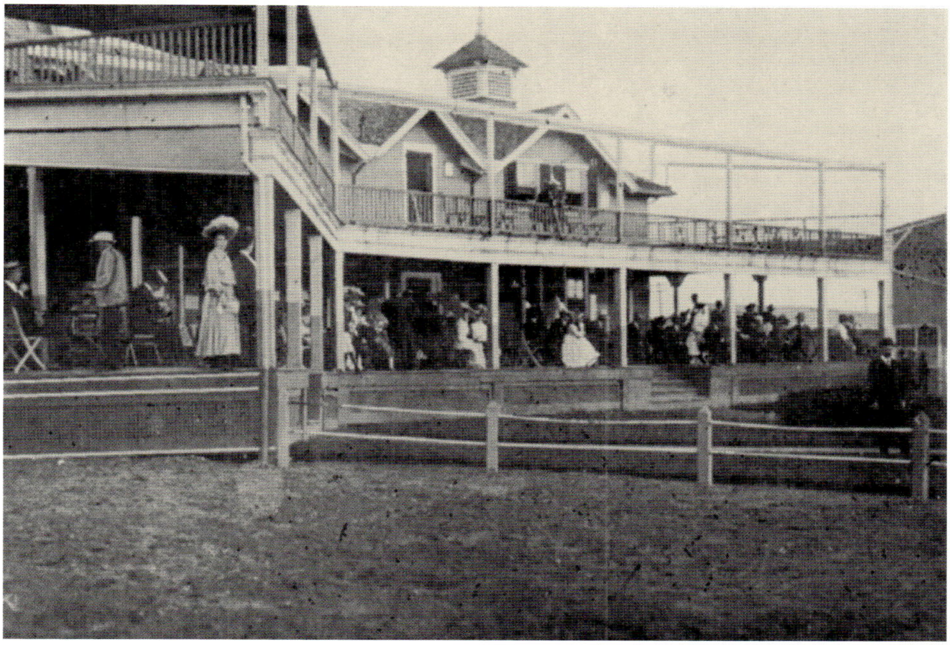

The Parkway Driving Club opened in 1892 on 25 acres bounded by Kings Highway, East Second Street, Quentin Road, and Ocean Parkway. It featured the genteel alternative of trotting to the more raucous horse races run at Gravesend's other tracks. Builder Henry Kornblum bought the site in 1921 and put up 300 one- and two-family homes there, ranging from $8,500 to $17,000. Kornblum named the development Ocean Gardens; predictably, he called another area project Parkway Gardens.

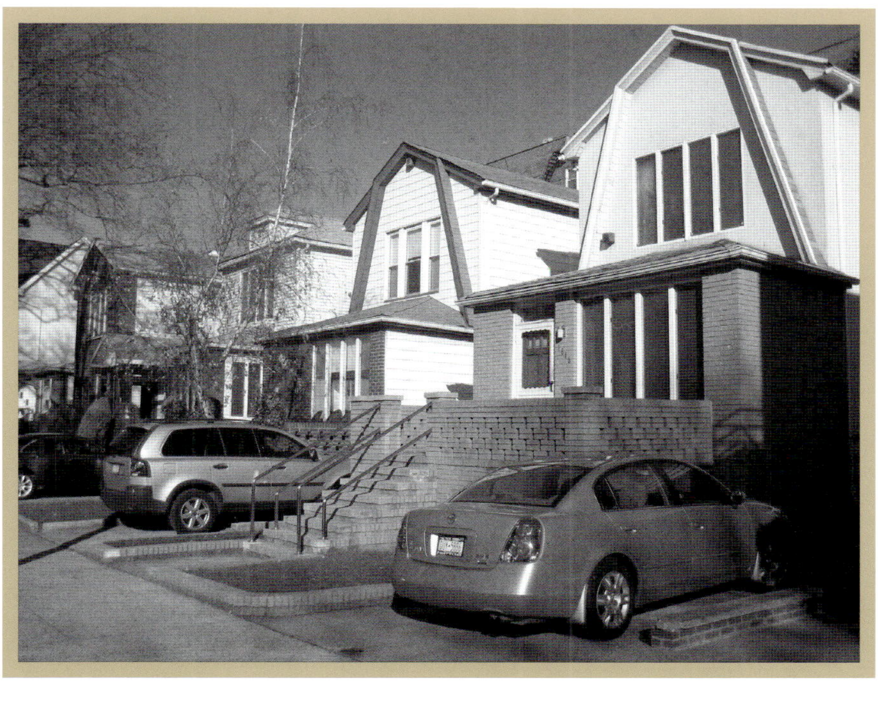

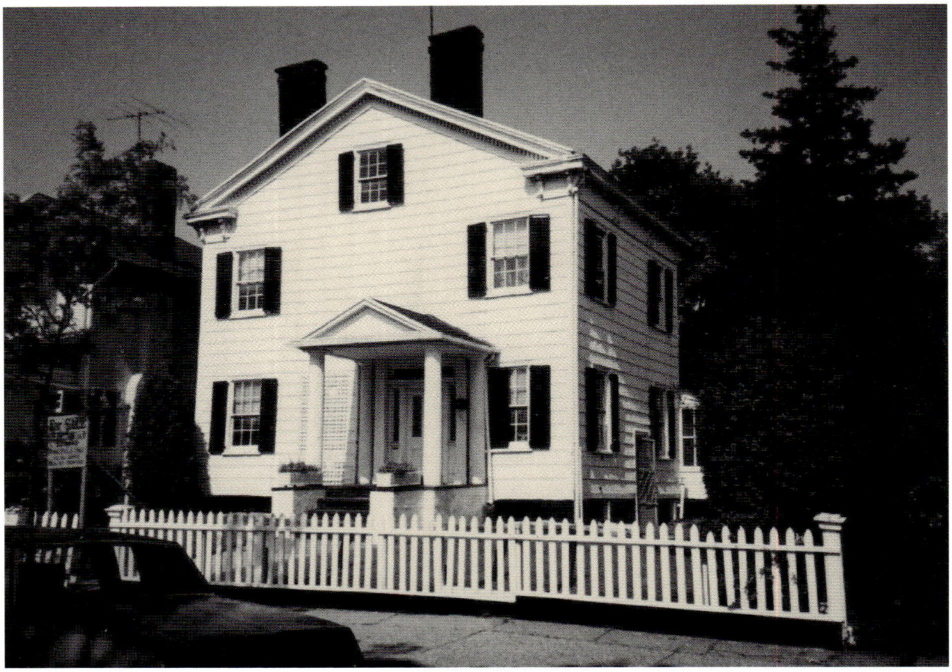

The Greek Revival–style house at 1637 Ocean Parkway stood originally at 929 Kings Highway, where it was home to William Van Brunt Bennett (1852–1914), last town supervisor of Gravesend. Erected around 1850, it was moved here in 1919 and turned 90 degrees to fit the narrow lot, its side becoming the street facade. Its similarity to the house on page 26 suggests both were built from the same pattern. It was replaced by the present home in 1994.

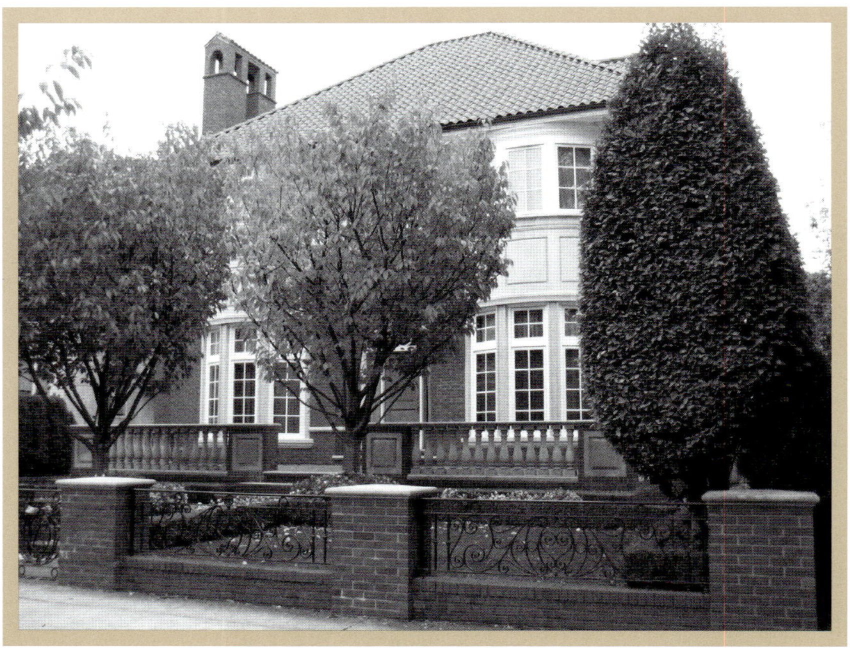

CHAPTER 3

WESTERN GRAVESEND

MARLBORO, ULMER PARK, AND CONEY ISLAND

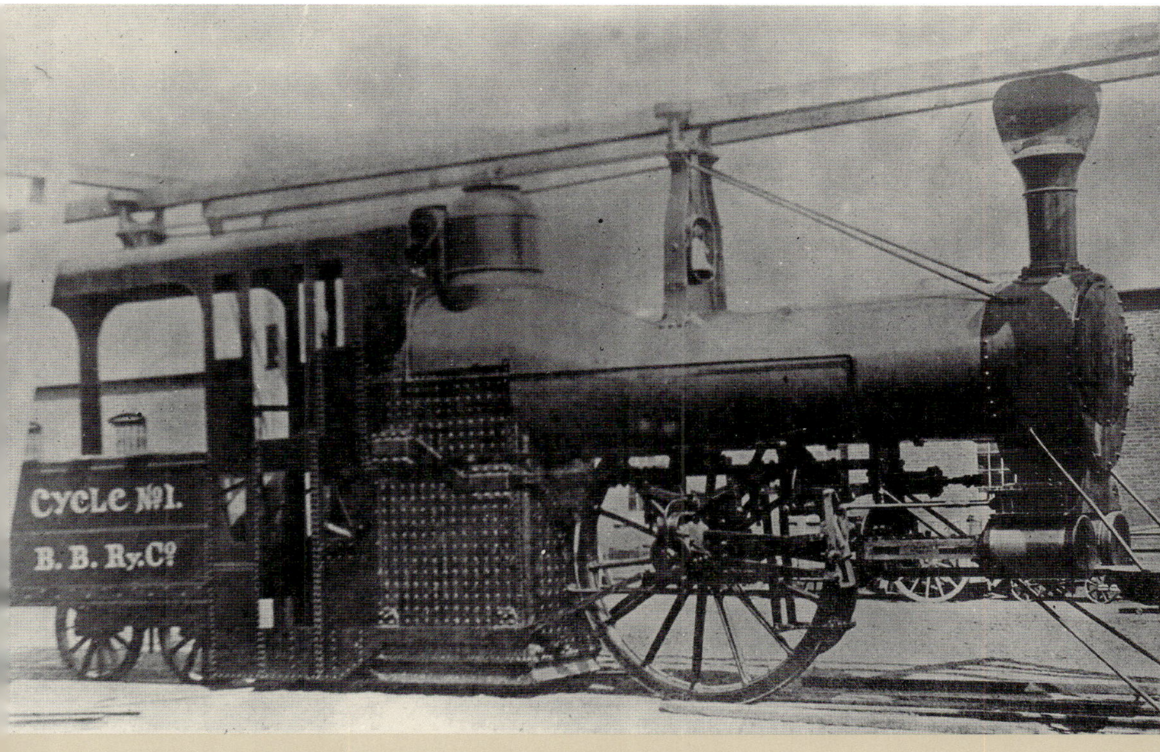

Block-long Boynton Place recalls inventor Eben Moody Boynton (1840–1927), whose improbable Bicycle Railway ran from there to Coney Island between 1889 and 1892. Boynton's train—a four-foot-wide car coupled to this equally narrow steam engine—traveled over a single rail on wheels set like a bicycle's, one behind the other. A guide above kept it from tipping over.

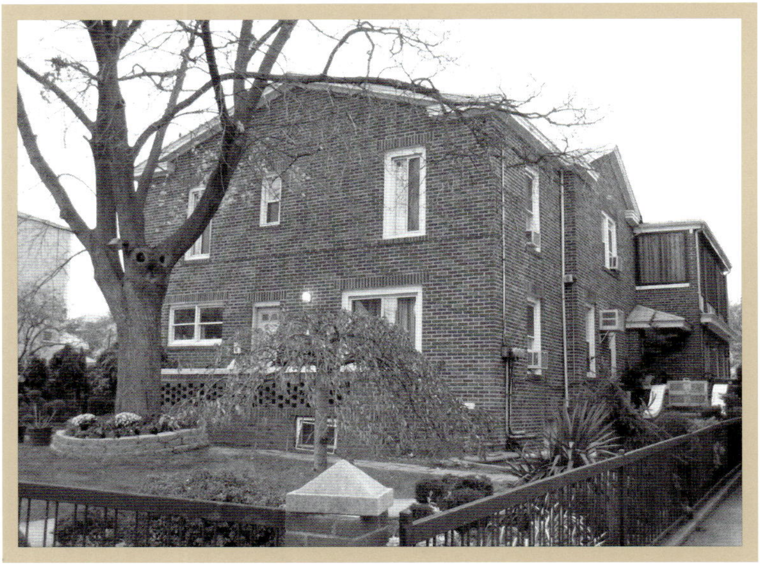

In 1861, longtime Gravesend town clerk Jacobus Lake (1824–1902) built this house at what became the northeast corner of West Sixth Street and Lake Place. The building, now designated 2157–2159 West Sixth Street, is unrecognizable under modern alterations. Lake Place was laid out by 1660 and originally divided two Lake family farms. It still runs east–west between Van Sicklen Street and Eighty-sixth Street, but adjacent property owners have recently fenced off its easternmost two blocks for private driveways.

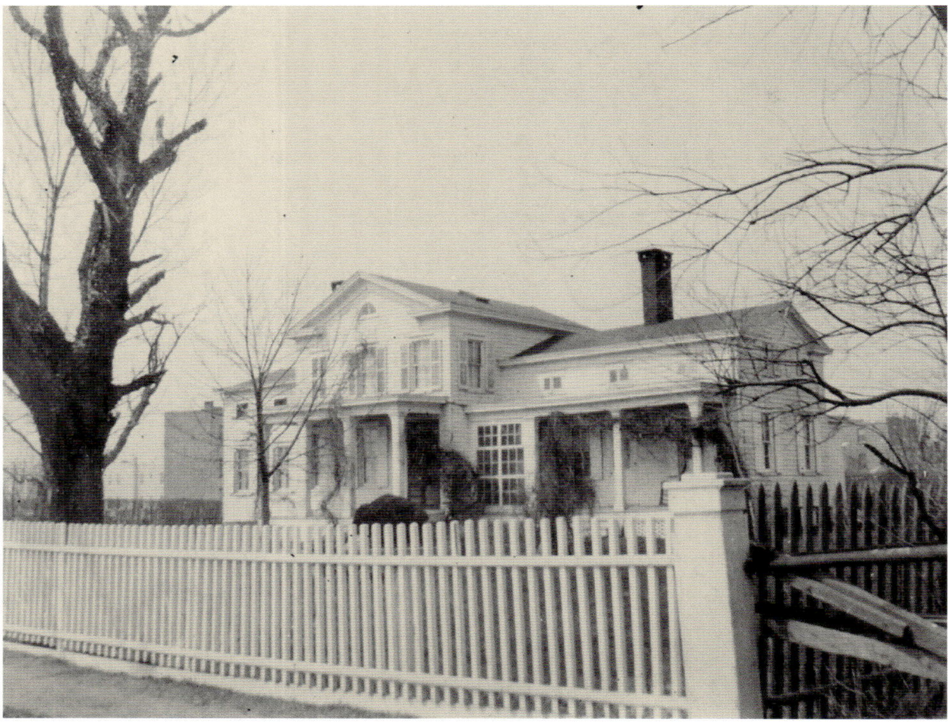

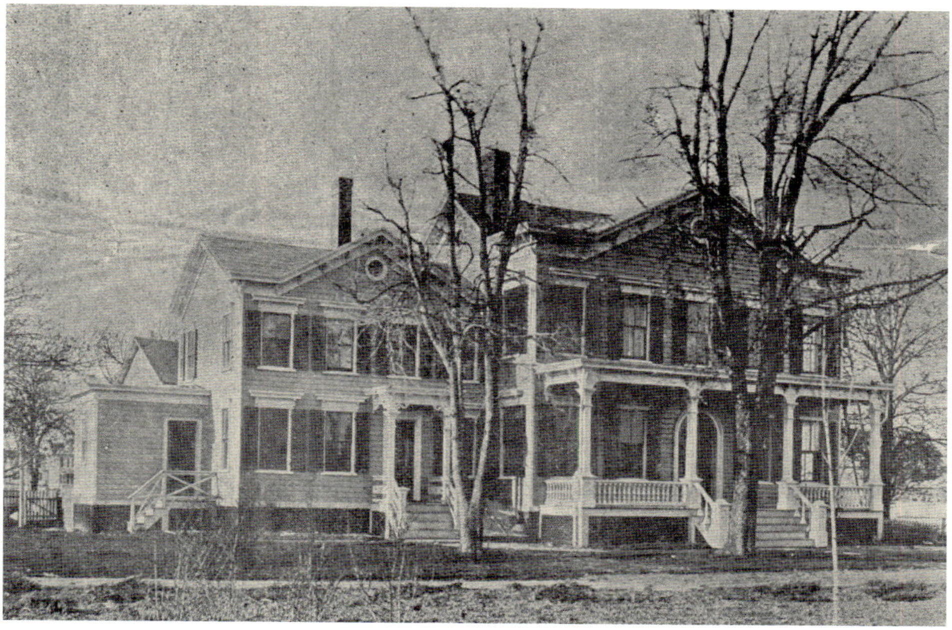

This dim historic image is one of the few taken of the 14-room house once located at 2063–2073 West Fifth Street. Built after 1884 by the carpenter James S. Voorhies (1838–1901), it replaced an earlier structure Charity Stryker sold to her son-in-law, David S. Jones, before 1876. The house was auctioned with 126 lots of surrounding Stryker farmland in 1901, but it stood as late as 1922 and probably survived until replaced by the present brick residences in 1928.

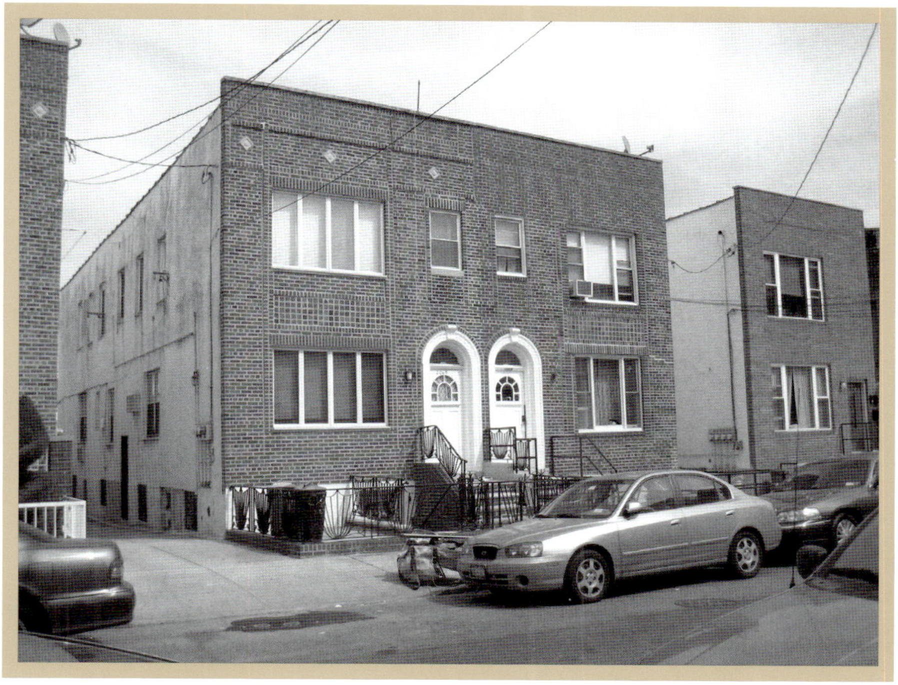

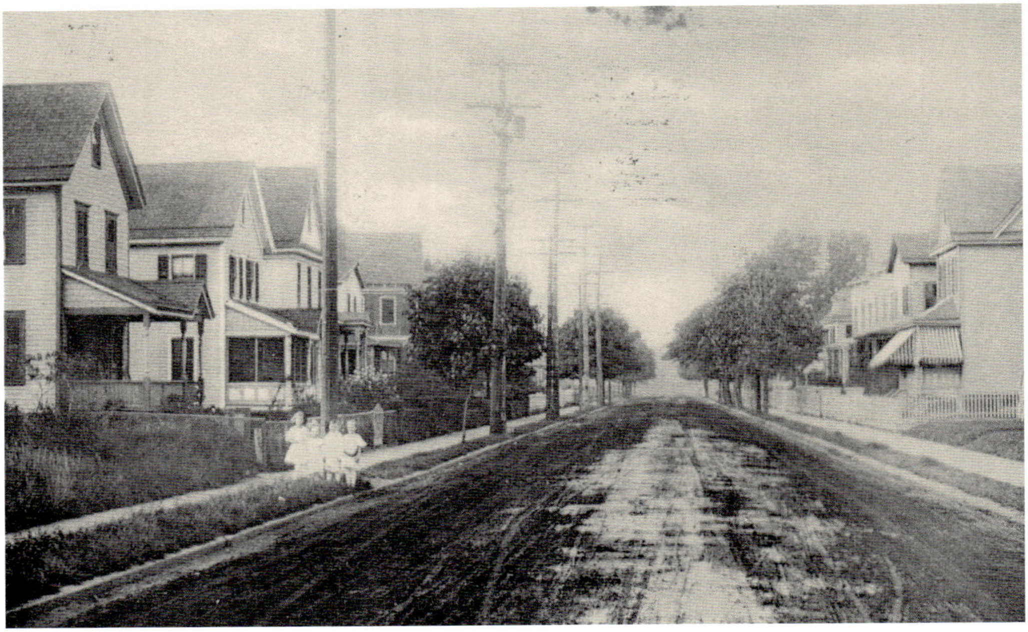

By the 20th century, descendants of Gravesend's early settlers were abandoning their ancestral farmhouses around the village square for new homes like these along Van Sicklen Street north of Avenue T. The two at the left, 194 and 190, are possibly those completed in 1899 by carpenter Peter Wyckoff Johnson (1833–1900) and described in the *Brooklyn Eagle* that July 30 as "costing $1,700 each and standing on plots 55 x 111 feet, in Van Sicklen Street, near Avenue T."

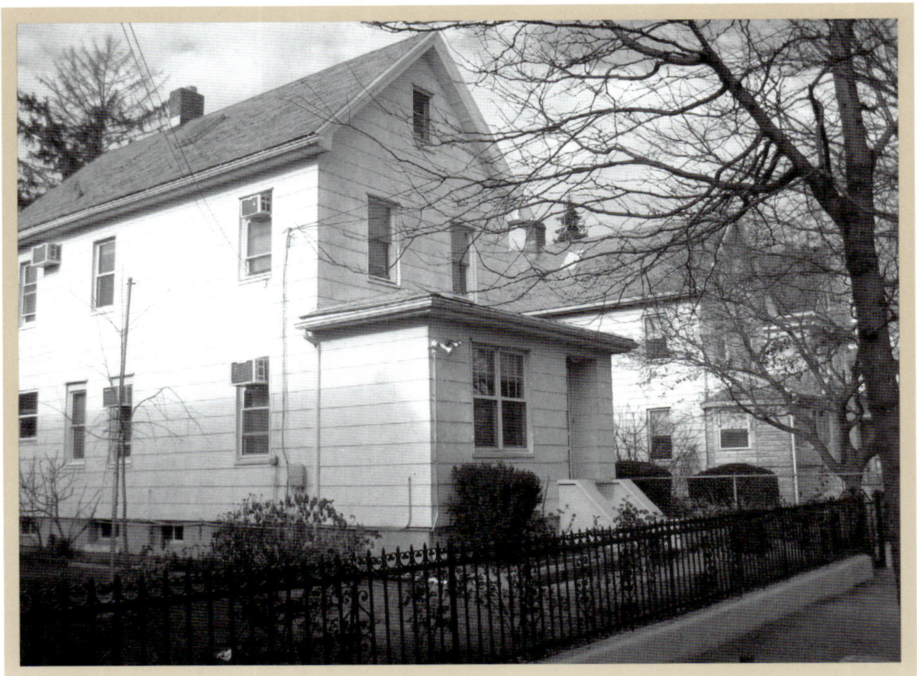

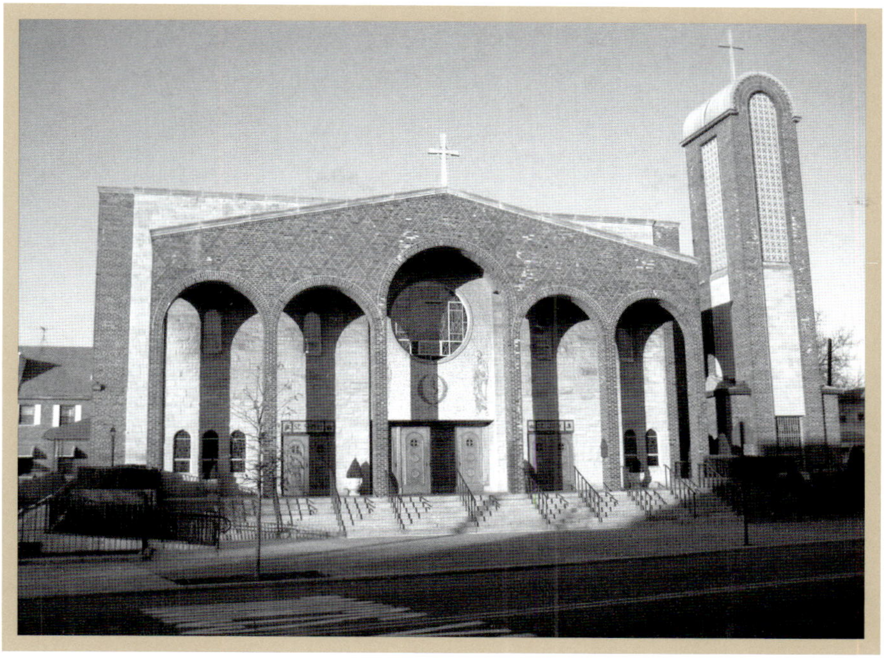

The first mass of the Roman Catholic parish of SS. Simon and Jude was celebrated in a barbershop at 321 Avenue T on Christmas Day, 1897. In 1898, the cornerstone for a permanent church was laid at the northeast corner of Van Sicklen Street and Avenue T; that sanctuary was consecrated in 1899. The current structure went up in 1966 on the site of the adjacent rectory, and the old church was demolished after the new one was dedicated in 1967.

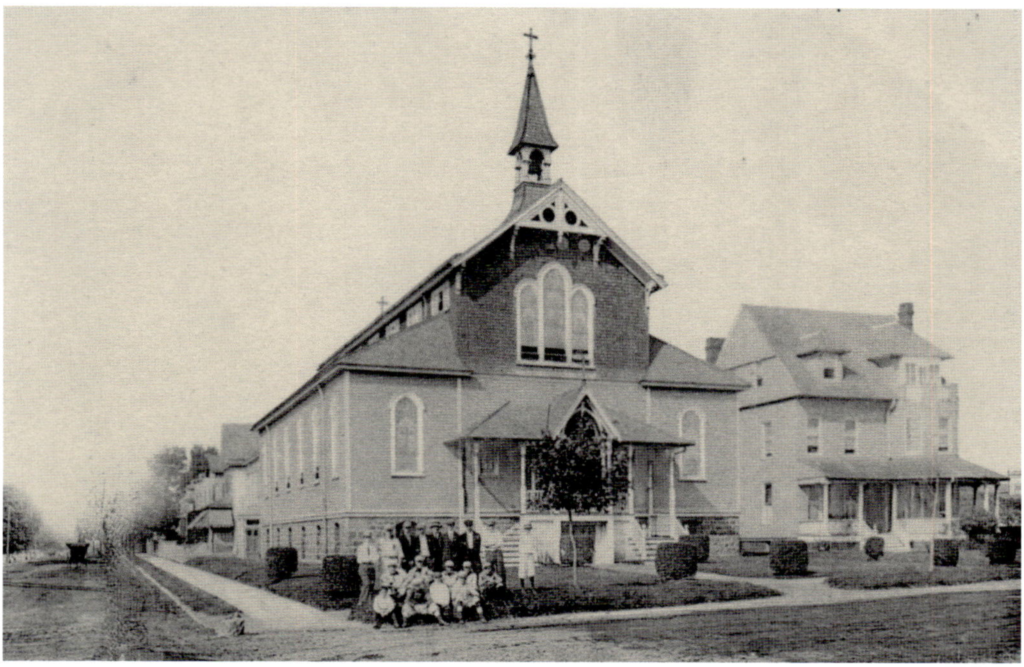

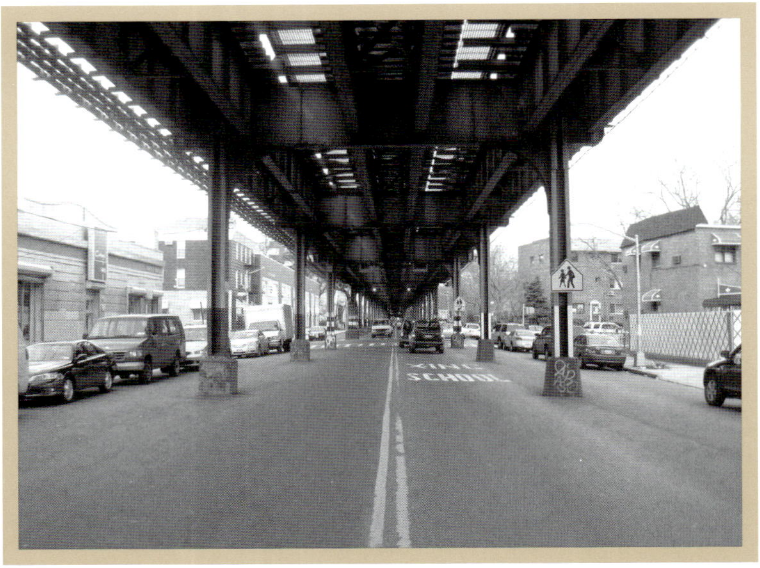

The central north–south road of Gravesend's village square was lengthened to Coney Island in 1824; that segment survives as Shell Road. A northern extension, known as Gravesend Avenue and shown here looking north to Avenue T, opened through New Utrecht and Flatbush in 1838. In 1933, it was renamed McDonald Avenue for John R. McDonald (1871–1932), chief clerk of the Kings County Surrogate's Court. The Culver Line Elevated, today's F train, has shaded the street since 1919.

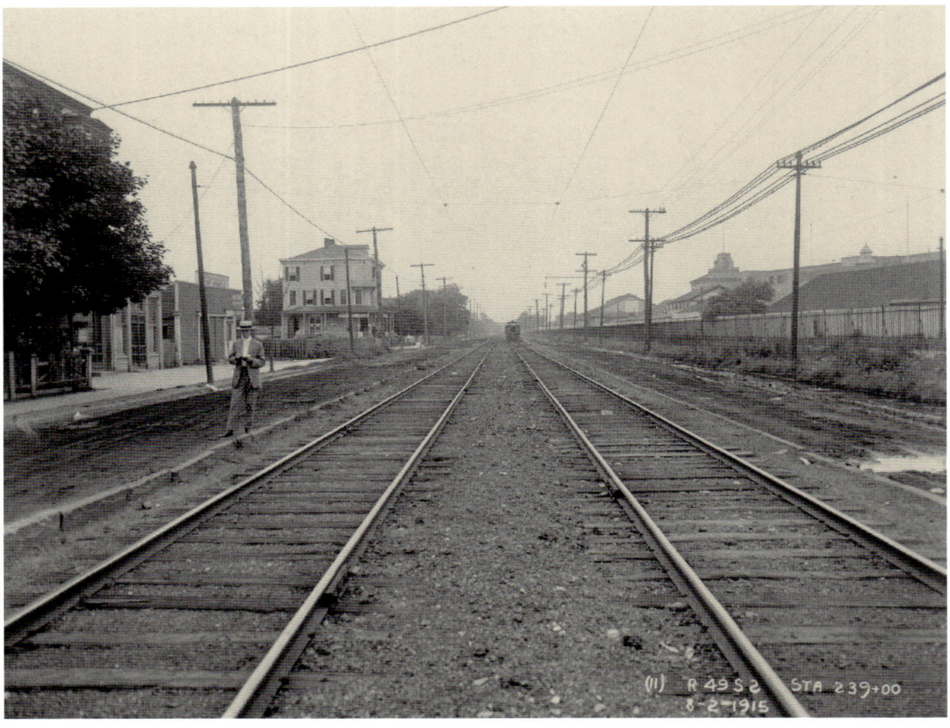

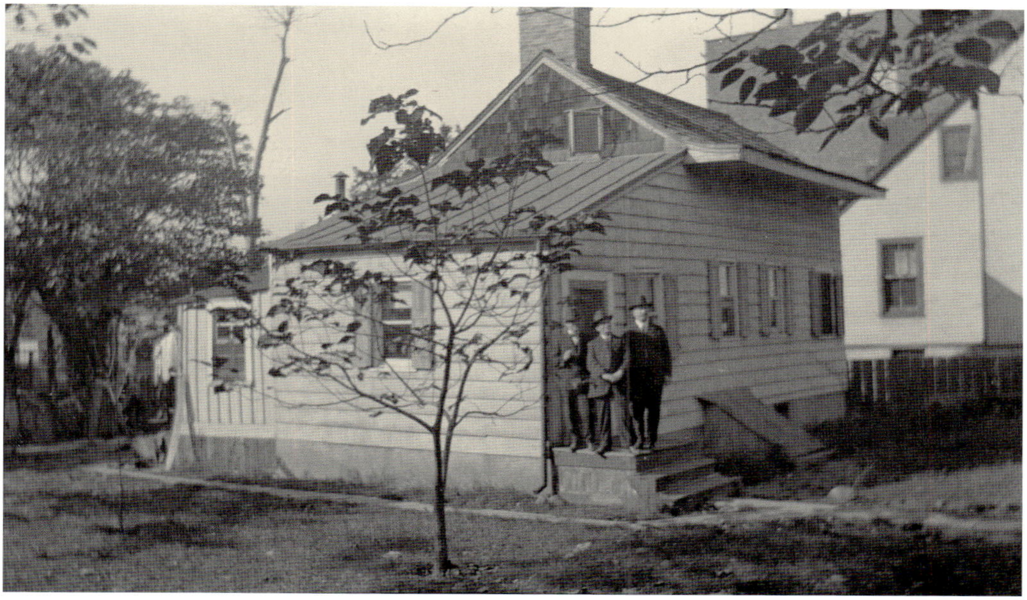

No. 2138 McDonald Avenue was built early in the 1830s for Nelly (Johnson) Hubbard, who occupied it briefly before moving to 2338 with her son, Samuel. Vincenzo Lucchelli bought the house in 1904 and added its two-story wing in 1924. His daughter Theresa (1901–1997) planted the towering catalpa tree on Arbor Day, around 1907. This smallest of Brooklyn's surviving Dutch houses was designated a New York City landmark in 2009. (Courtesy of John Antonides.)

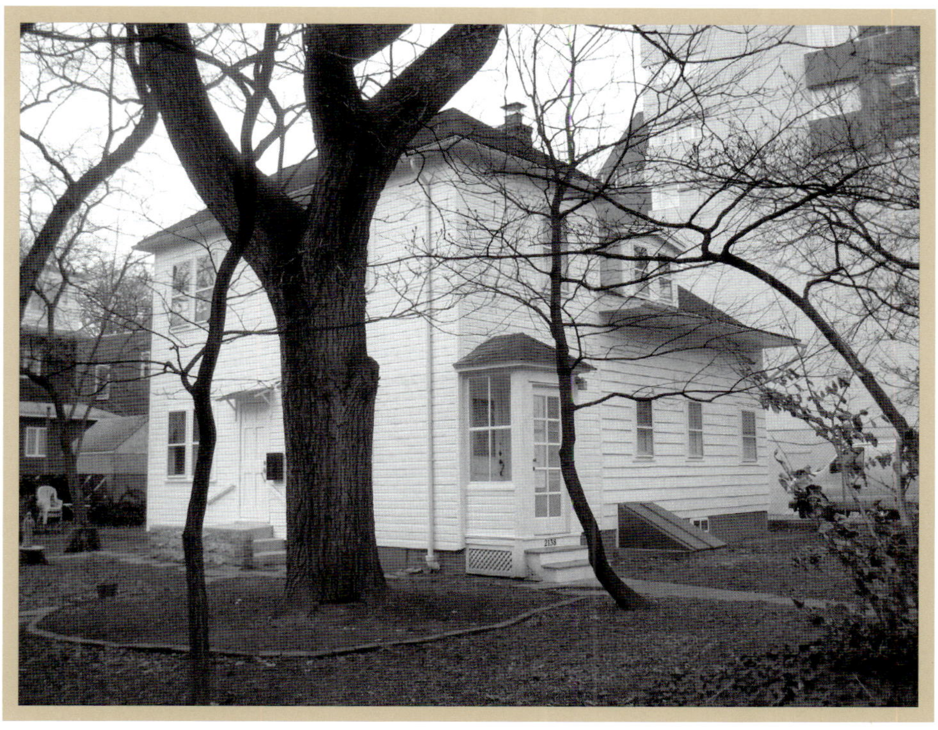

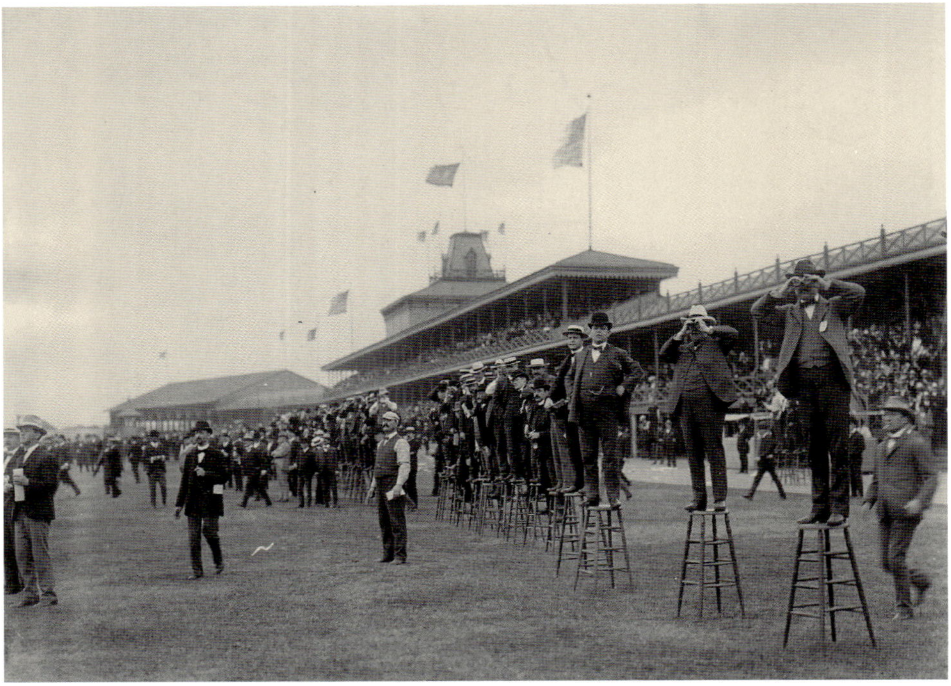

In 1886, the Brooklyn Jockey Club opened a mile-long racetrack bounded by Kings Highway, Ocean Parkway, Johnson's Lane (defunct), and McDonald Avenue. Its grandstand, seen here in 1902, bordered McDonald Avenue between Avenues S and T. The track closed when New York outlawed betting in 1910 and never reopened after the ban was lifted in 1913. The grandstand came down soon after 1920, when realtor William E. Harmon bought the site for development as the Kings Club District.

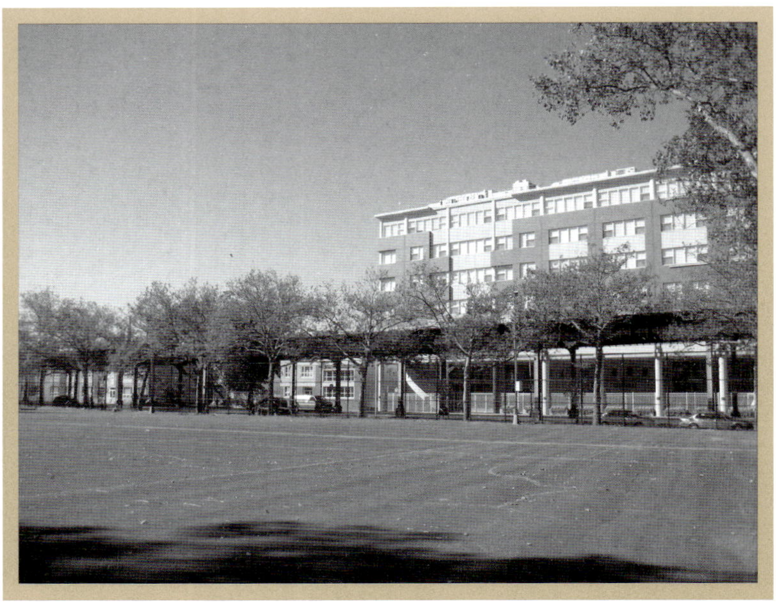

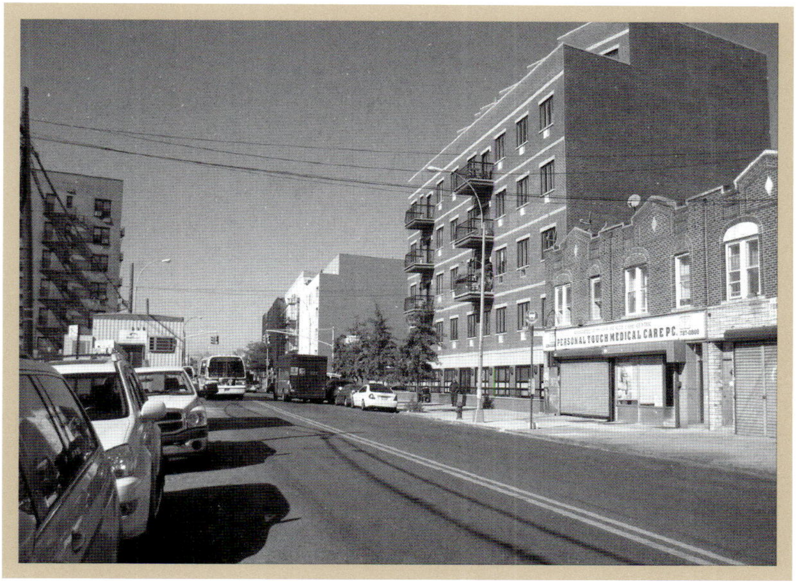

The otherwise orderly street grid of modern southern Brooklyn retains some historic anomalies. One was ancient even to the Native Americans, who called it Mechawanienk, meaning "old path or trail." In the 17th century, it connected the European settlements on southwestern Long Island. By 1704, the British were using this road to carry the royal mail. Kings Highway, shown here in 1922 with the Dutch-style Stillwell house at No. 359, still follows the winding route of the former footpath.

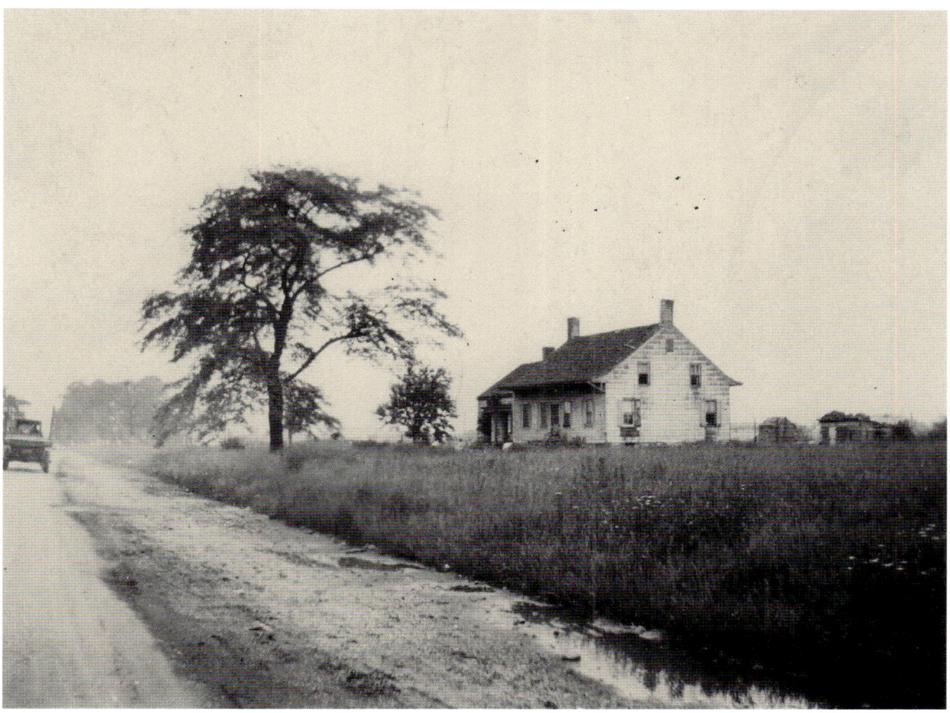

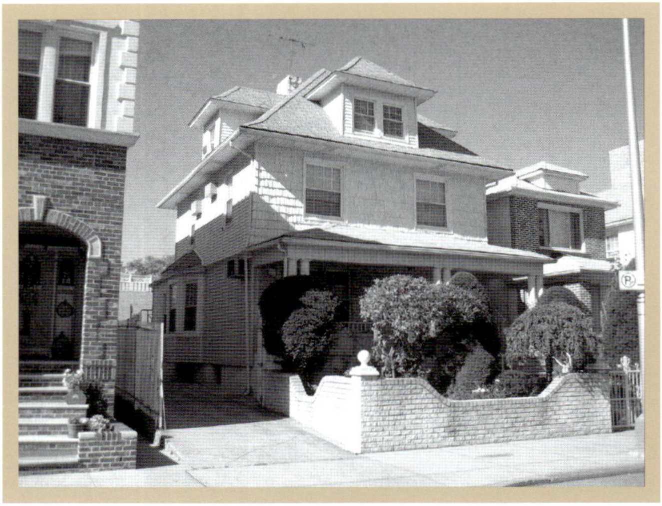

In 1902, realtors Wood, Harmon and Company deployed crews to "uproot the beets and turnips and demolish the antiquated farm buildings" on the recently acquired property they named Marlboro. The tract was bounded by Sixtieth Street, Bay Parkway, Avenue P, and McDonald Avenue. Street grading followed the initial transformation, and homes, like this one for lawyer Charles F. Catlin at 1572 West Third Street, were ready for occupancy by 1904. (Courtesy of the New-York Historical Society.)

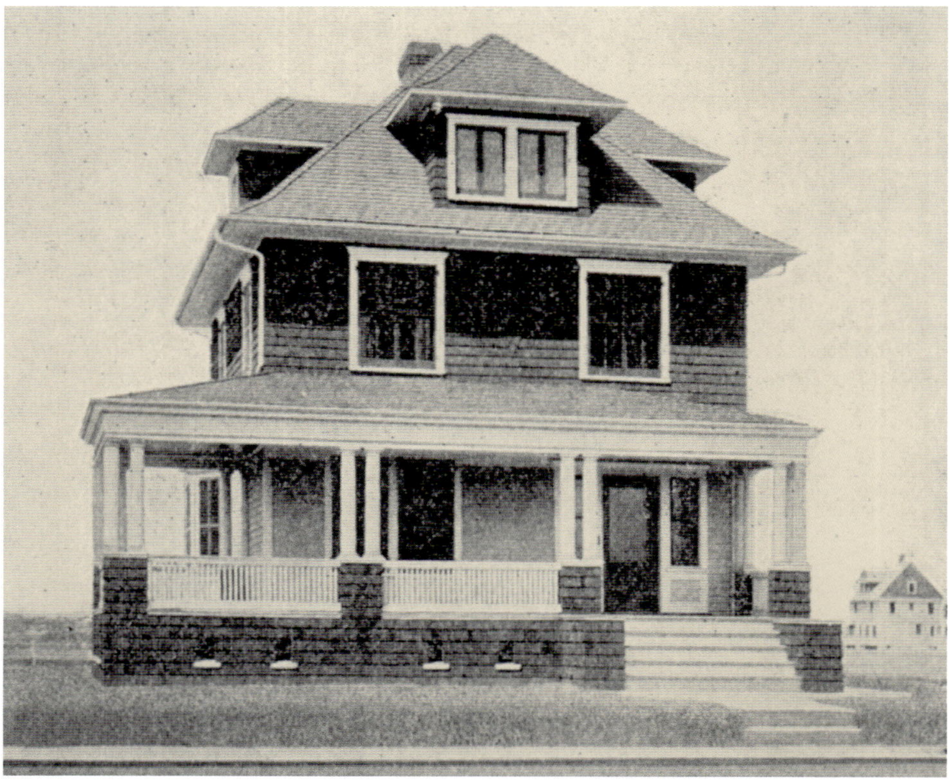

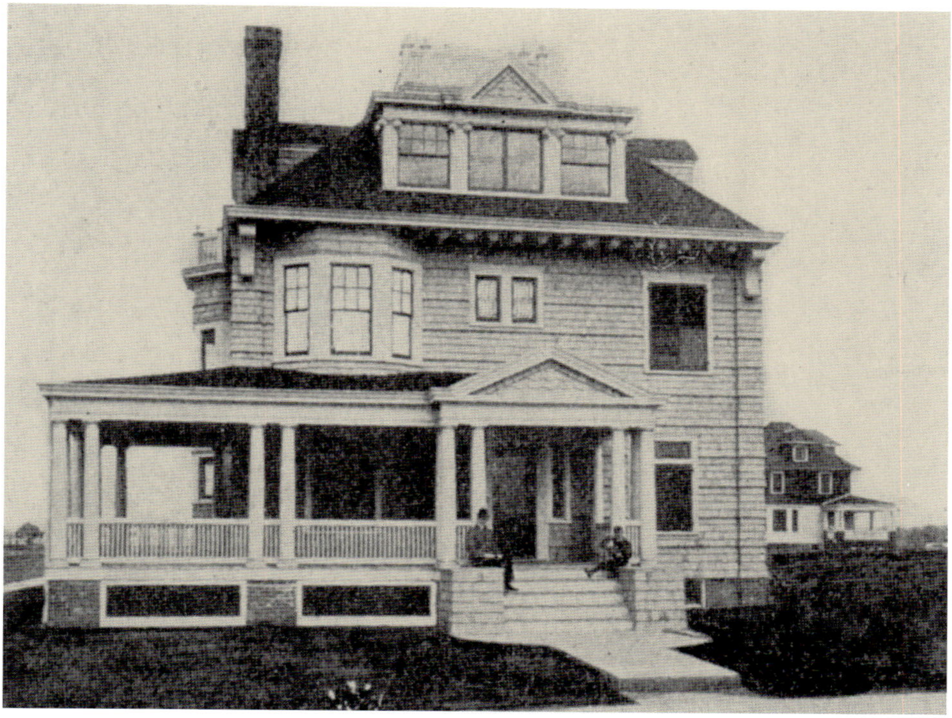

Developers Wood, Harmon and Company predicted in 1903 that Marlboro would soon "present a magnificent park-like appearance . . . cross-marked into squares by the regular, well-kept streets and dotted here and there by handsome houses." Among the first erected was the $11,150 home at 273 Avenue P. Dow C. Smith, superintendent of the Brooklyn Rapid Transit Company, bought it in 1905, but the house stood just 30 years longer until demolished for the current apartment building. (Courtesy of the New-York Historical Society.)

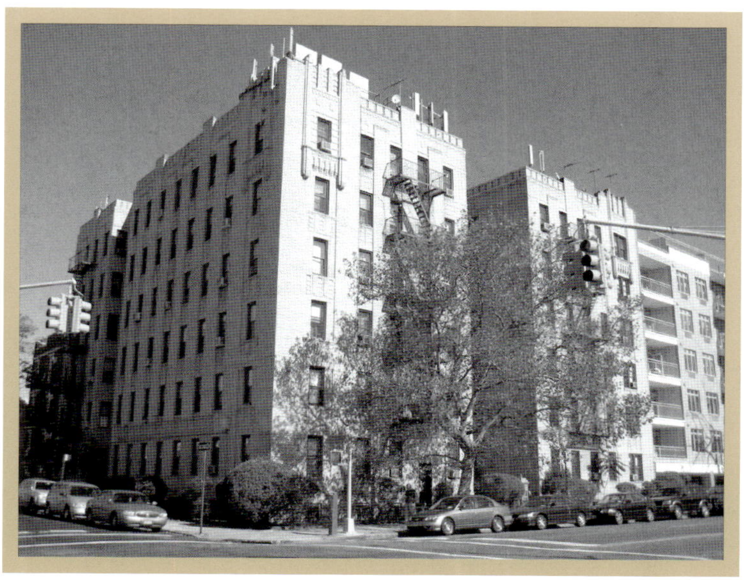

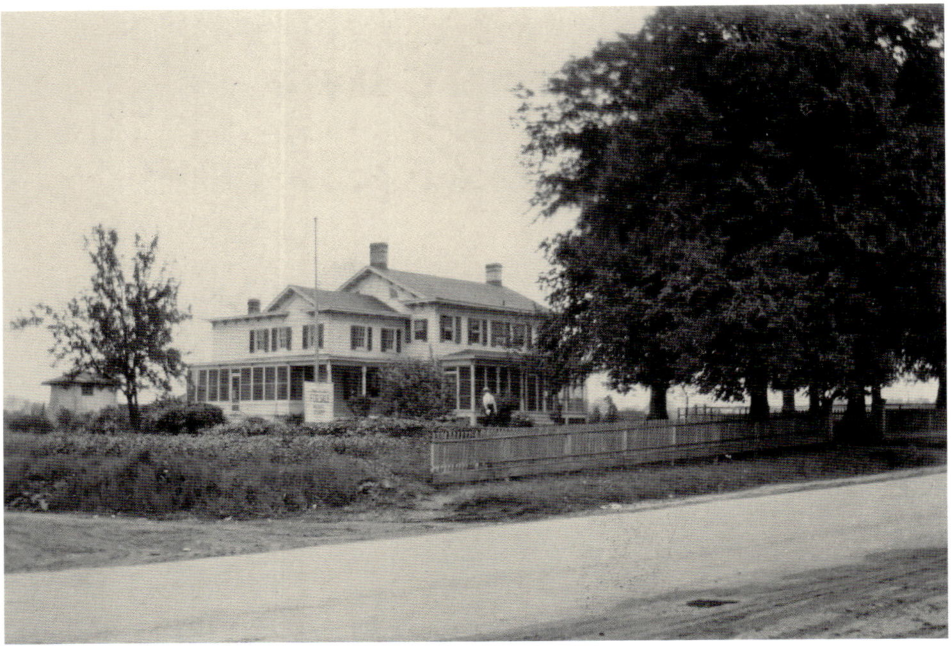

John Stillwell Bennett (1856–1938) learned to drive a car late in life, handling it like a horse by yelling "Whoa there!" He farmed 40 acres north of his house at 289 Kings Highway, but sold the property to developers around 1922. The Sommer Highway Theatre opened on the site in 1925 and closed about 60 years later; it was demolished in 2008. An apartment house around the corner at 1702 West Sixth Street—the Bennett Arms—recalls the former landowner.

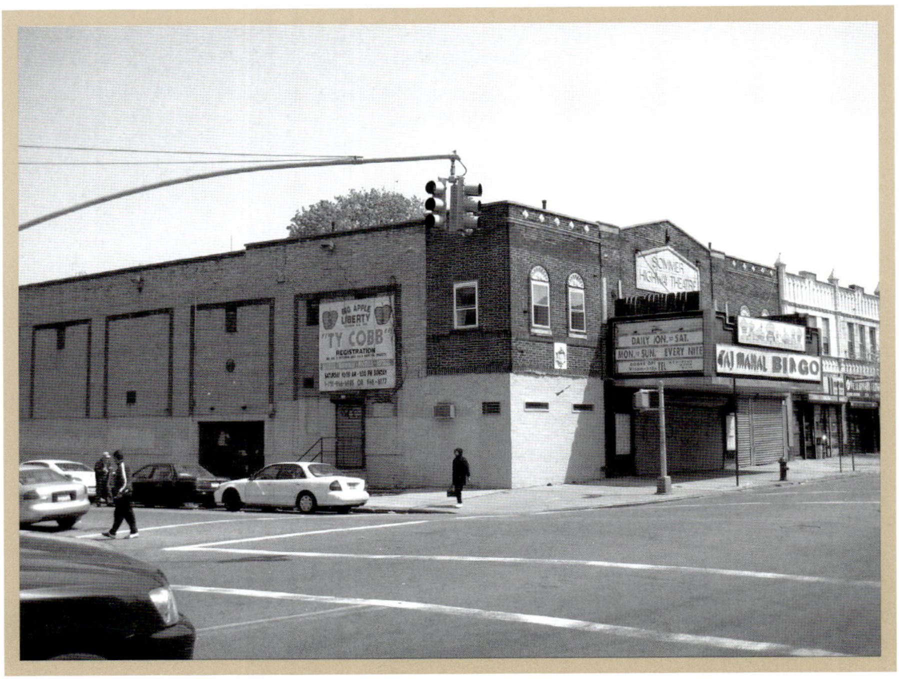

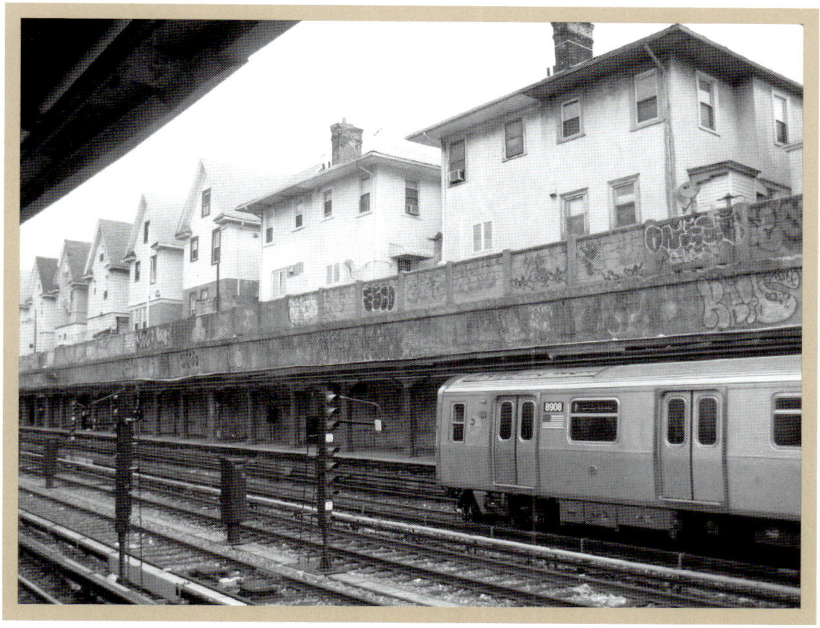

In 1879, the New York and Sea Beach Railroad, precursor of today's N train, opened from Bay Ridge to the Sea Beach Palace, its hotel-terminus on Surf Avenue, Coney Island. The line was electrified in 1898 and set in its present four-track cut between 1913 and 1915. In 1914, the houses at 1754–1800 West Seventh Street, seen here abutting the right-of-way north of Highlawn Avenue, were propped up while workers carved out the Manhattan-bound platform of the Kings Highway Station.

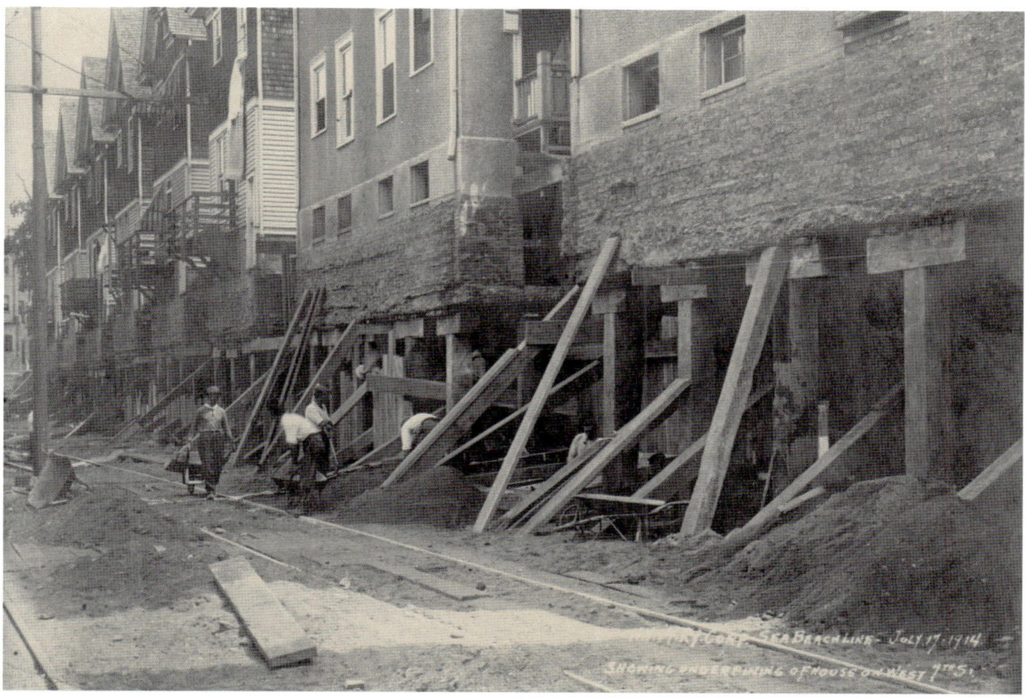

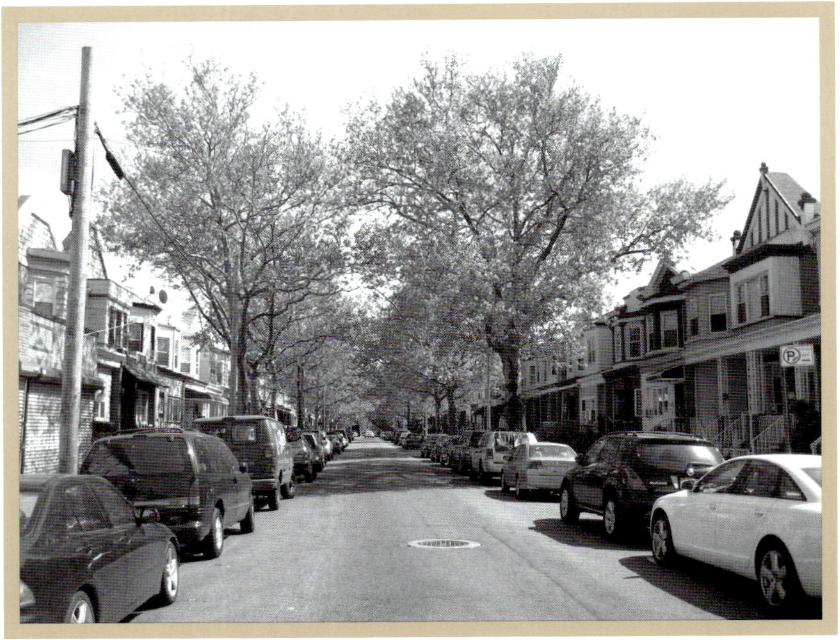

Real estate developer Otto Singer (1866–1928) built several rows of speculative model homes in Gravesend before World War I. In 1909, he advertised these on the 1700 block of West Eighth Street, south of Kings Highway. They featured seven rooms with hardwood trim plus bath and laundry for $4,750 ($300 down, $16 per month). Porches have been enclosed and some decorative gables removed or covered by siding, but Singer's houses remain essentially intact a century after they went up.

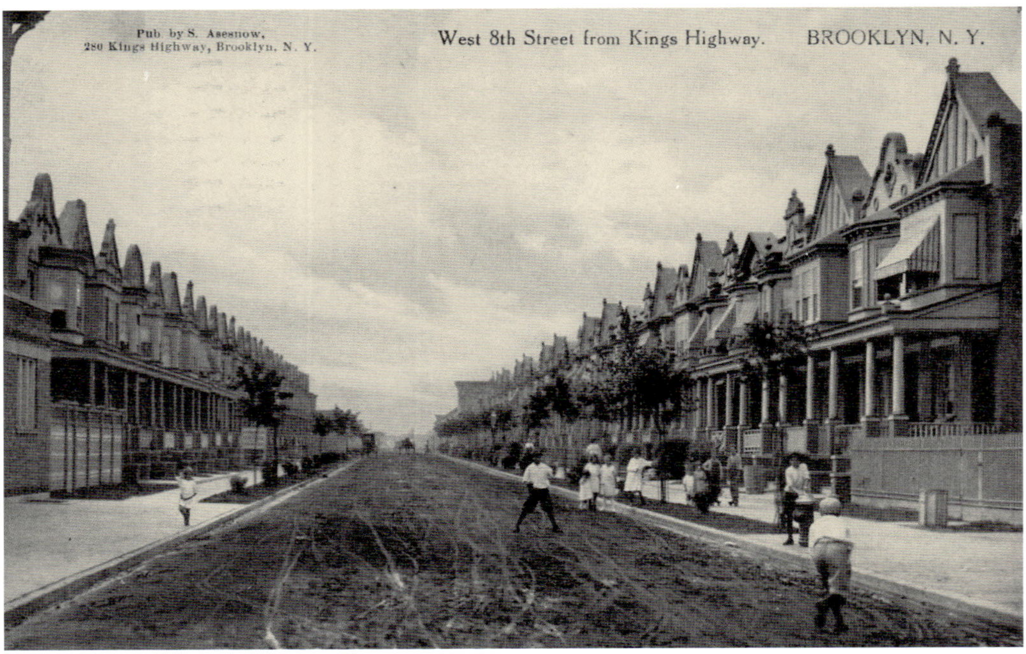

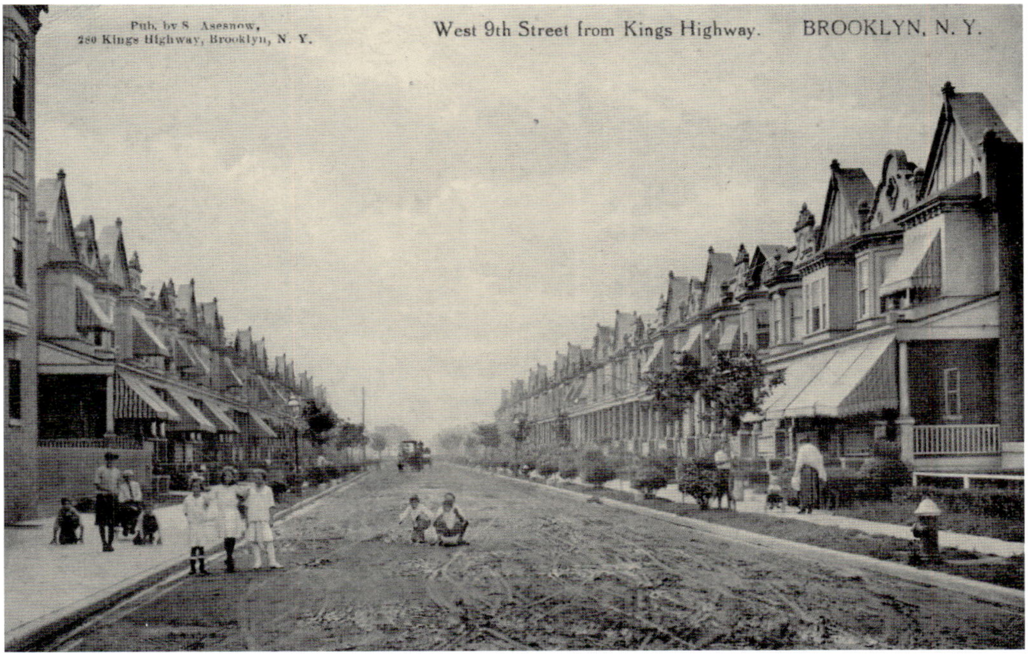

The fanciful roofline ornamentation on Otto Singer's model homes adds rhythmic interest to what are basically 17-foot-wide, nondescript brick houses. The two rows shown here lining West Ninth Street between Kings Highway and Highlawn Avenue are identical to those a block over on West Eighth. In all, there are 131 Singer homes on both streets. They sold quickly when new due to the proximity of the Sea Beach Subway Line (today's N train).

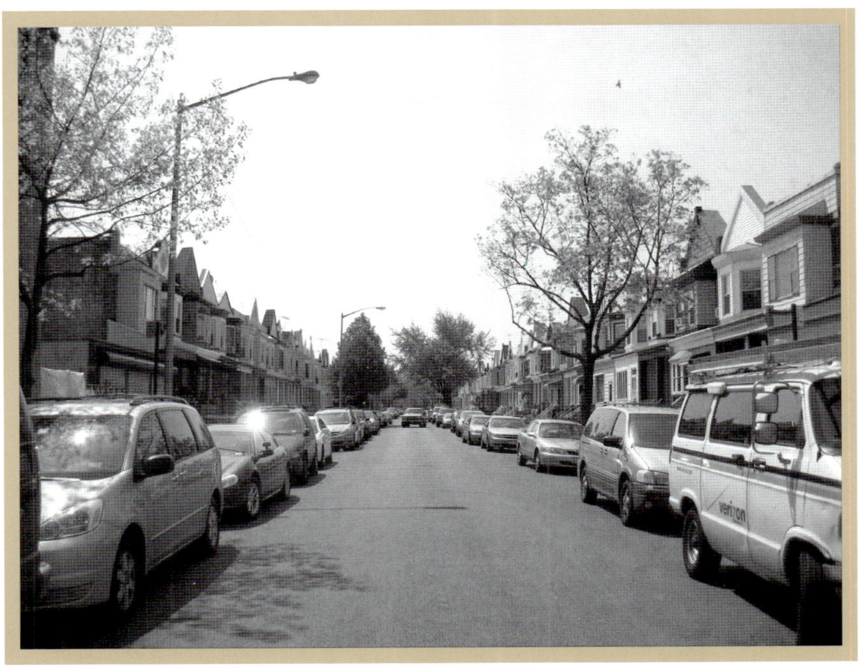

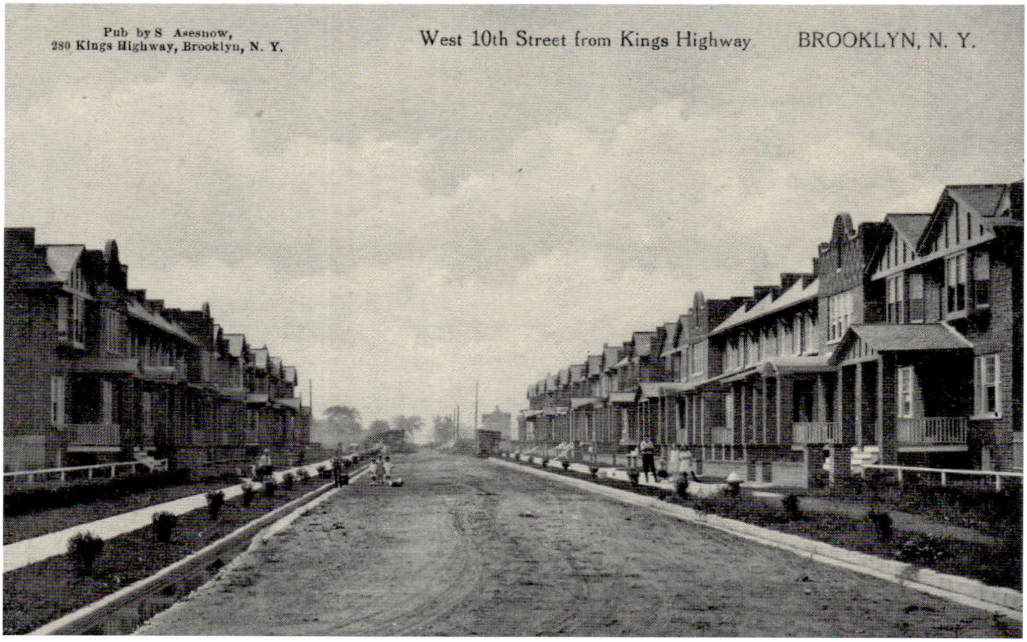

Designed in muted shades of "tapestry brick" on the 1700 block of West Tenth Street, Otto Singer's Old English Dwellings were first advertised in 1913. Unlike his earlier homes on West Eighth and Ninth Streets, which run in unbroken rows, Singer built these in short groups with a concession to the growing presence of cars in Gravesend: driveways between the corner houses. The builder himself occupied No. 1755, the semi-detached model in the current photograph.

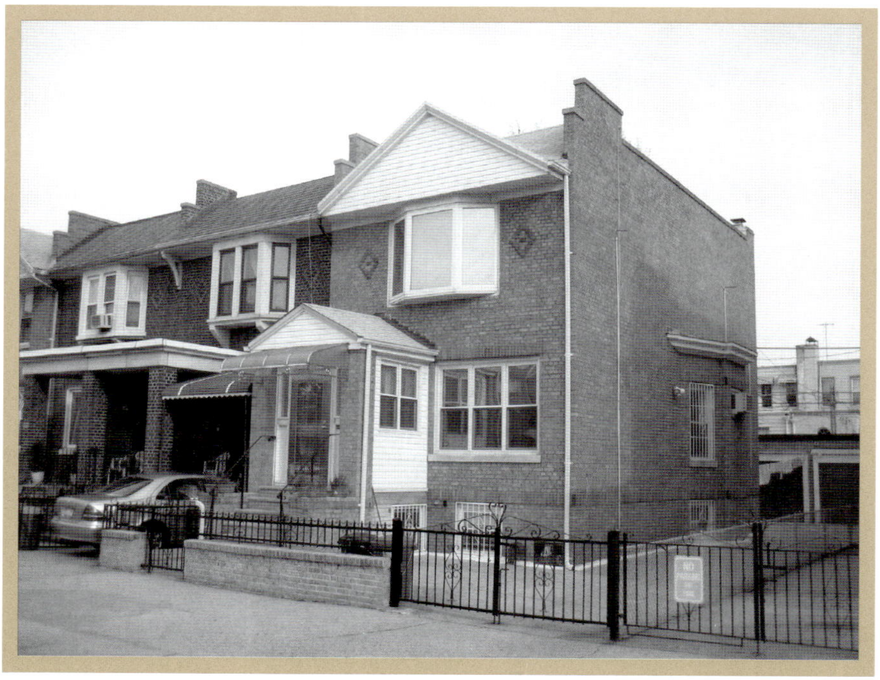

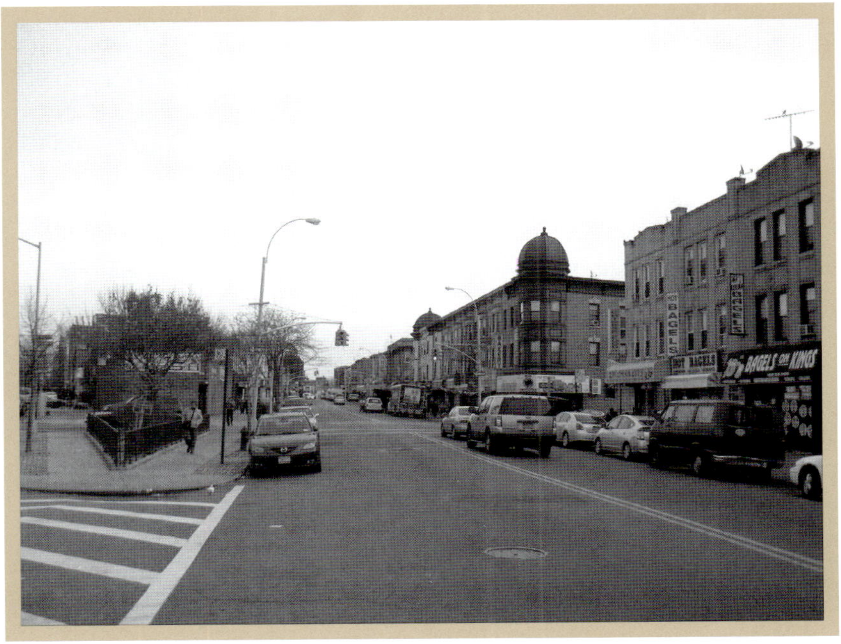

The old image here, from a possibly unique postcard mailed in 1915, captures Gravesend in transition. The view is east down Kings Highway from West Tenth Street. On the left spread fields and the homestead of John Stillwell Bennett. On the right, capped by corner domes, stands the recently built row of three-story brick flats at 236–256 Kings Highway. For the moment, poised in opposition across the unpaved road, Gravesend, the farming town, faces its urban future.

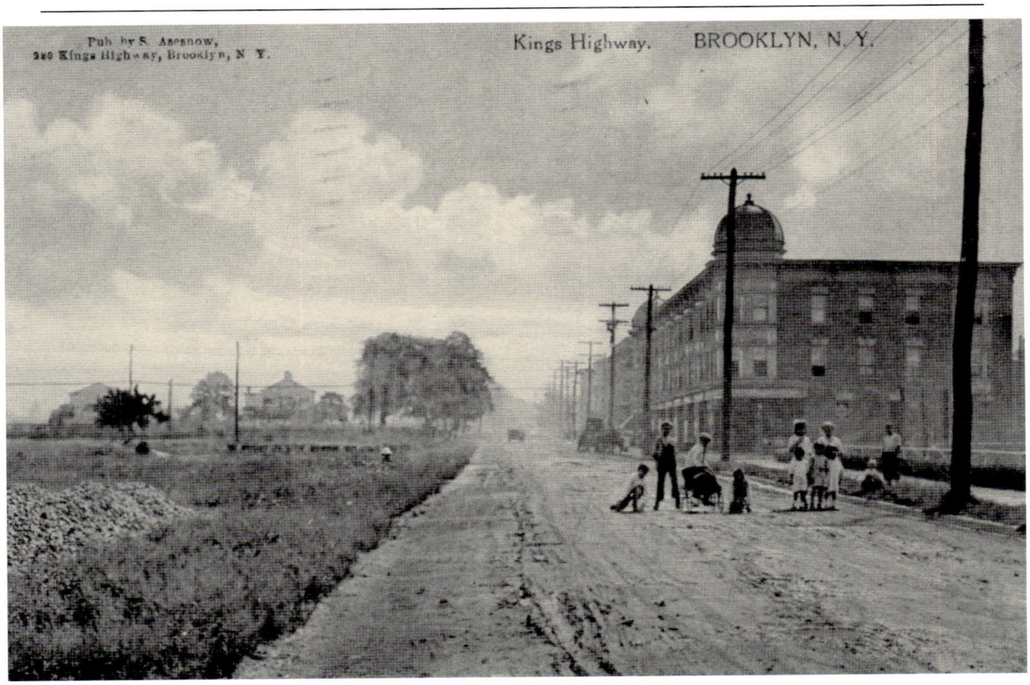

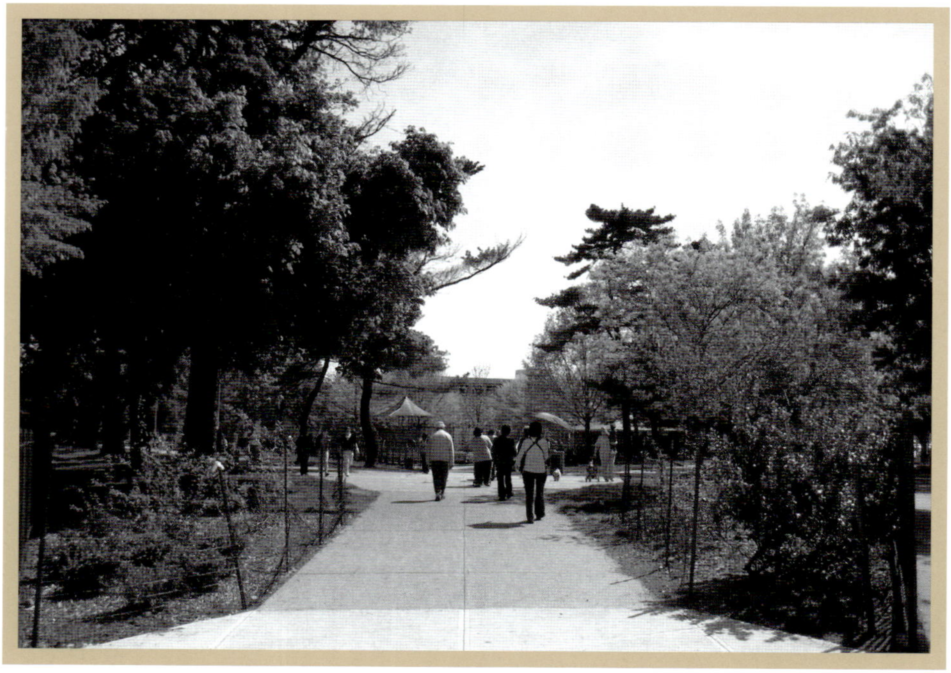

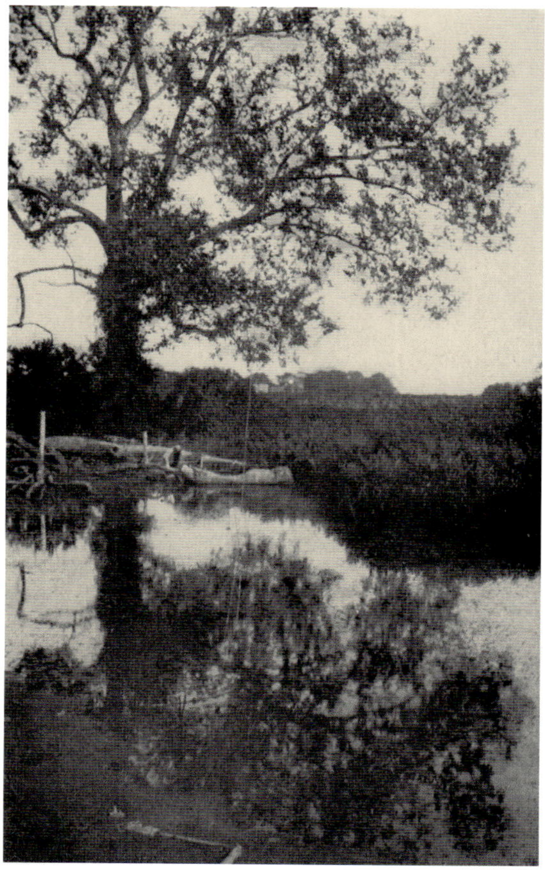

The 1645 patent for Gravesend set the town's boundaries by natural landmarks, among them "a Certaine pond in an ould Indian field." Indian Pond, as it came to be called, covered 31 acres where Avenue P meets Stillwell Avenue. Its name echoed former nearby settlements of Upper Delawaran Native Americans. As Brooklyn grew around it early in the 20th century, Indian Pond filled with garbage until it went dry. In 1924, part of its site became Seth Low Playground.

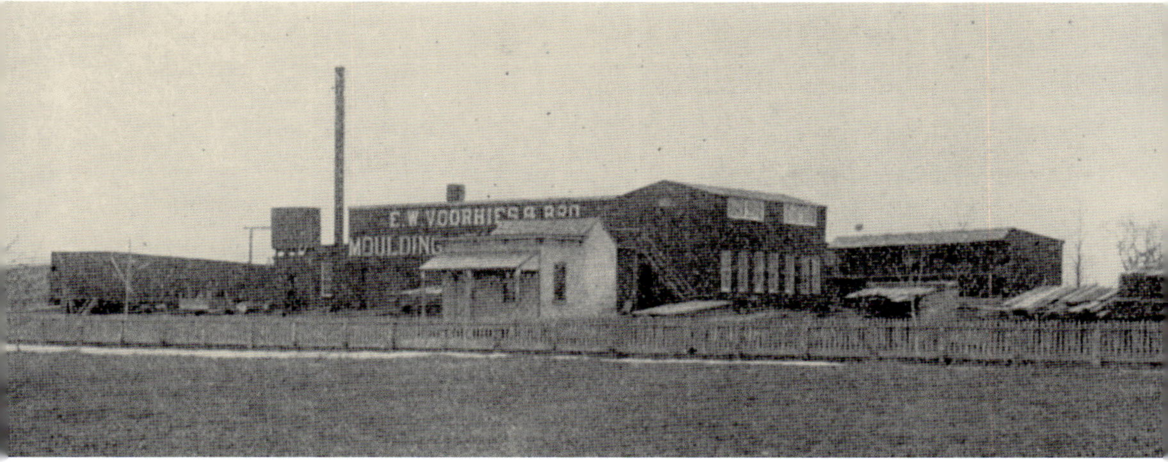

From their planing mill, established in 1890 on the north side of Avenue S between West Ninth and Tenth Streets, brothers Edmond W. (1865–1949) and Henry V. D. Voorhies (1856–1924) supplied moldings, boards, trim, brackets, turned work, and window sashes—the basic lumber carpenters used to frame Gravesend's present building stock. Most of the area's one- and two-family homes and occasional apartment houses went up before 1929. By then, even the Voorhies mill had been replaced with residences.

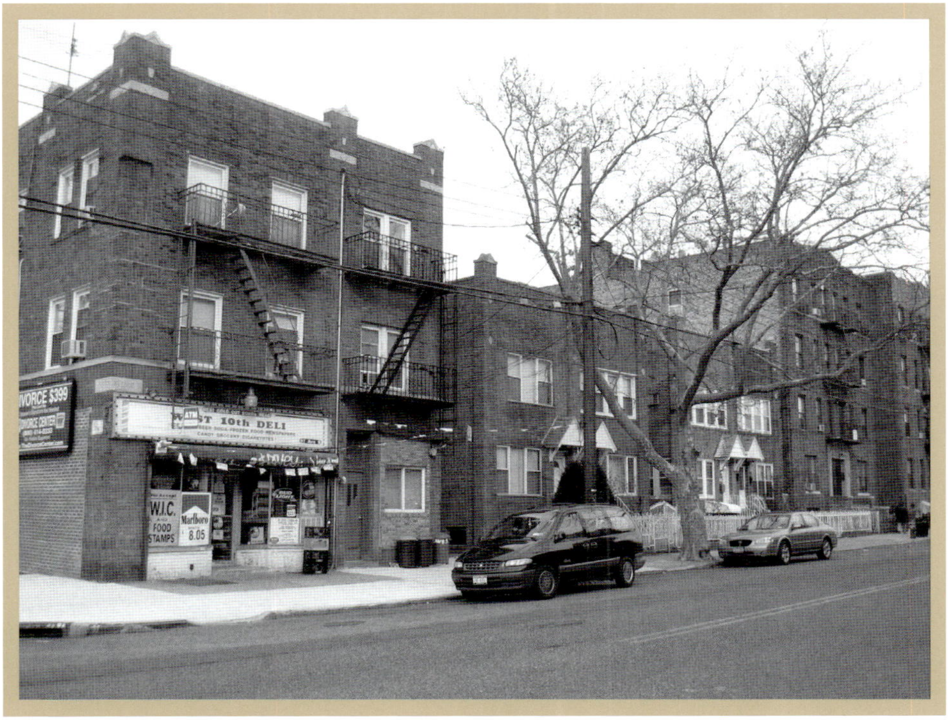

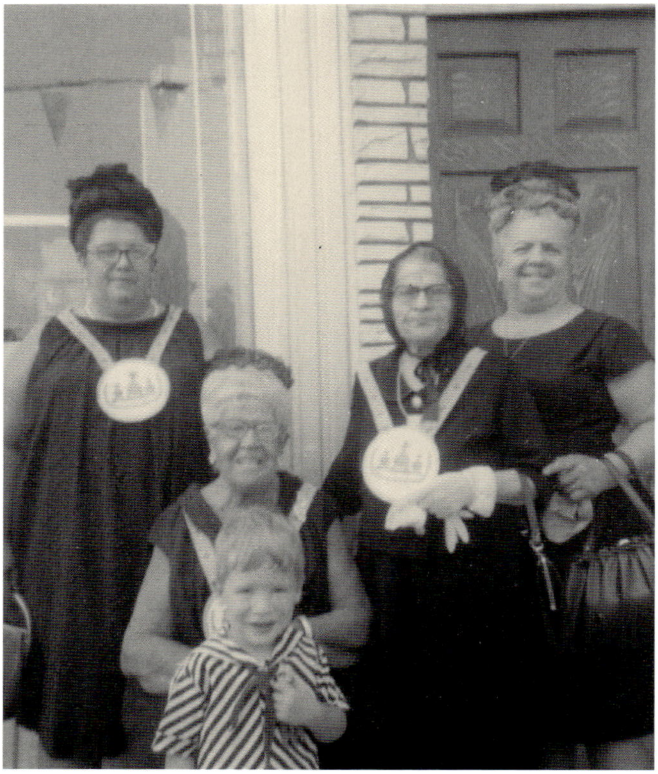

Italian immigrants from the town of Bisceglie, Bari, left crowded lower Manhattan for Gravesend in the 1920s and 1930s. They established a mutual aid society and in 1932 built a function hall at 49 Avenue T (now the Gesher Yehuda Orthodox Jewish School). Here four members of the Ladies' Society, SS. Martiri di Bisceglie (with the author), pose around 1970 outside their headquarters at 118 Avenue T. Much of Gravesend's Italian population has since moved to Staten Island and beyond.

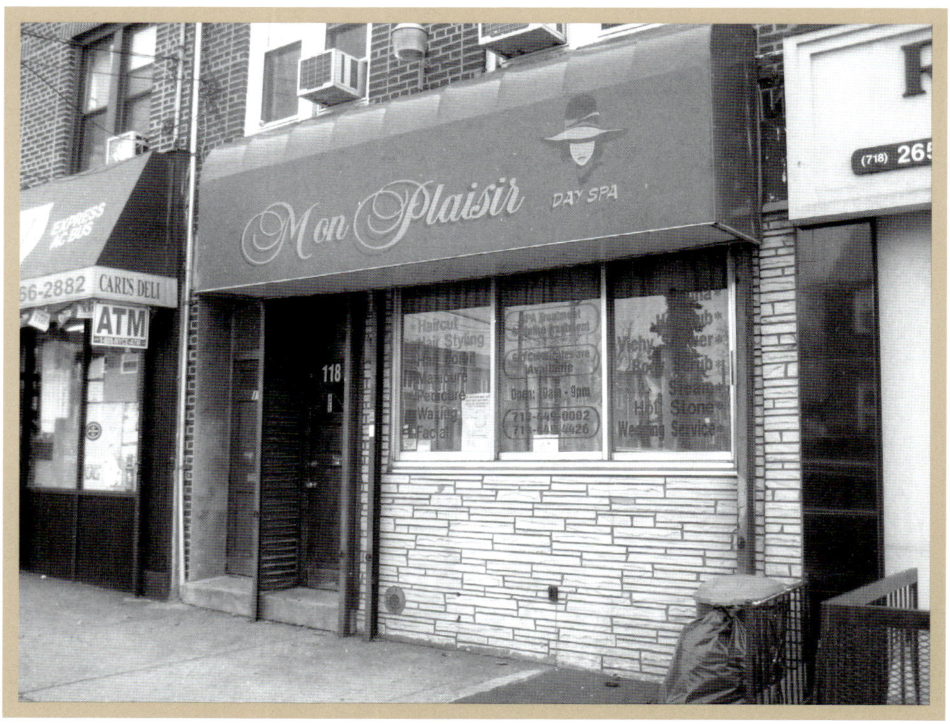

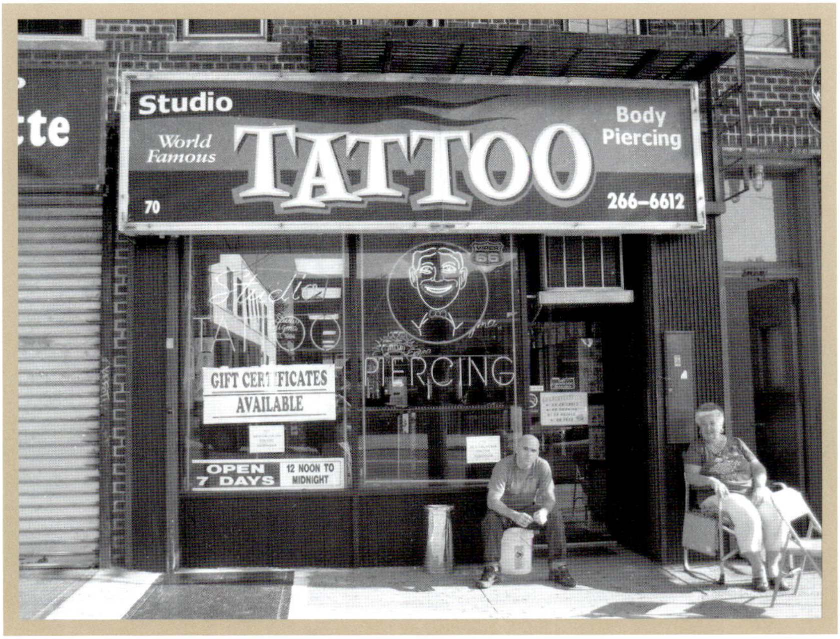

In the *c.* 1949 photograph, Armando Varacalli (1908–1979) poses in the grocery store established by his father, Giuseppe, at 70 Avenue U. Advertisements for beers once brewed in Brooklyn hang around the well-stocked shop: Rheingold, Schaefer, Trommer's, and Piel's. Armando's heirs ran the business after he died, but the store closed early in the 1990s. After a stint as a pet-supply shop, the space became the popular tattoo parlor it remains today. (Courtesy of the Varacalli family.)

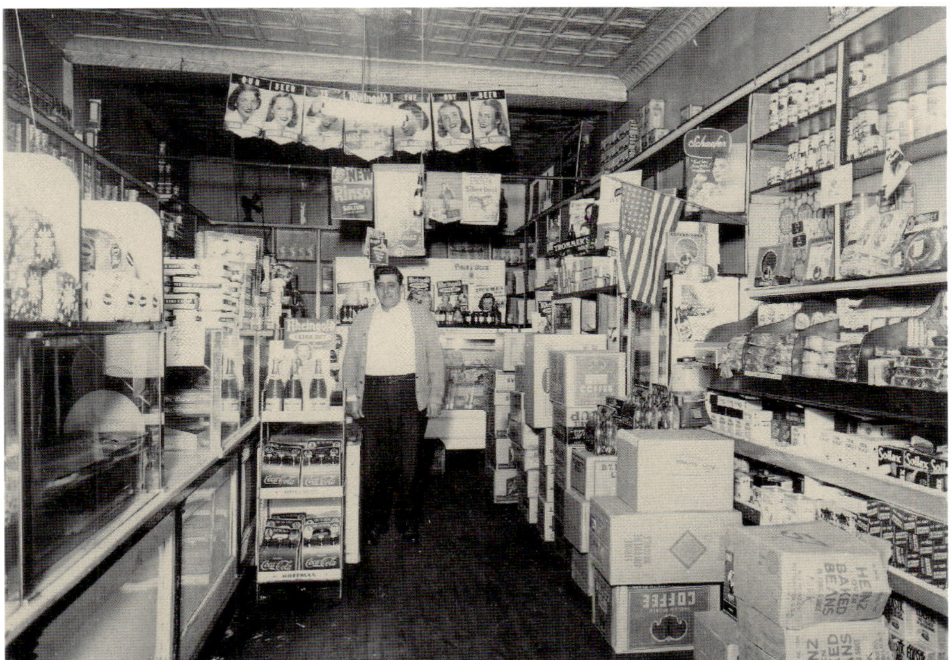

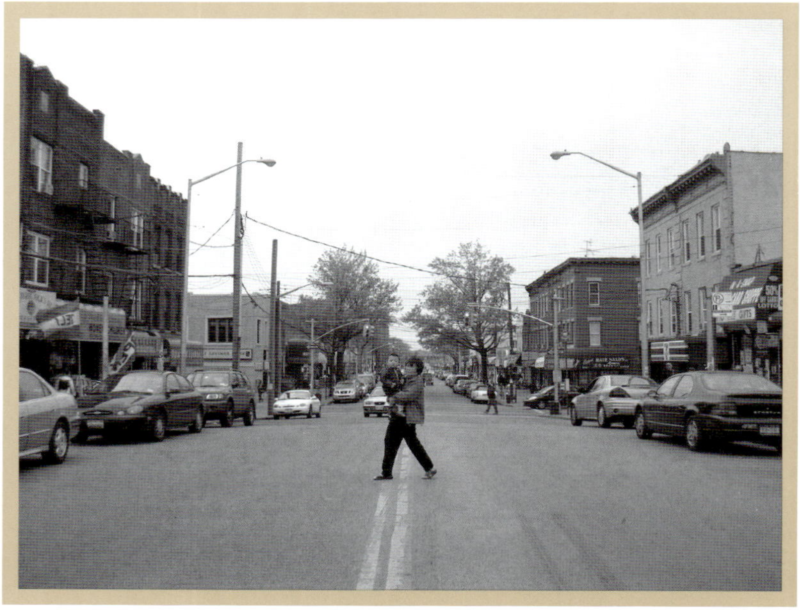

After initial opposition from adjoining property owners, Avenue U opened through Gravesend in 1896. The 80-foot-wide, macadamized road spanned three miles between Eighty-sixth Street and Gerritsen's Creek. Contemporary real estate advertisements praised the "splendid new parkway," which gave smooth access compared to earlier rutted lanes. In 1914, the stretch west of West Seventh Street was dug up for sewer installation while work progressed to set the Sea Beach Subway tracks, today's N train, below street level.

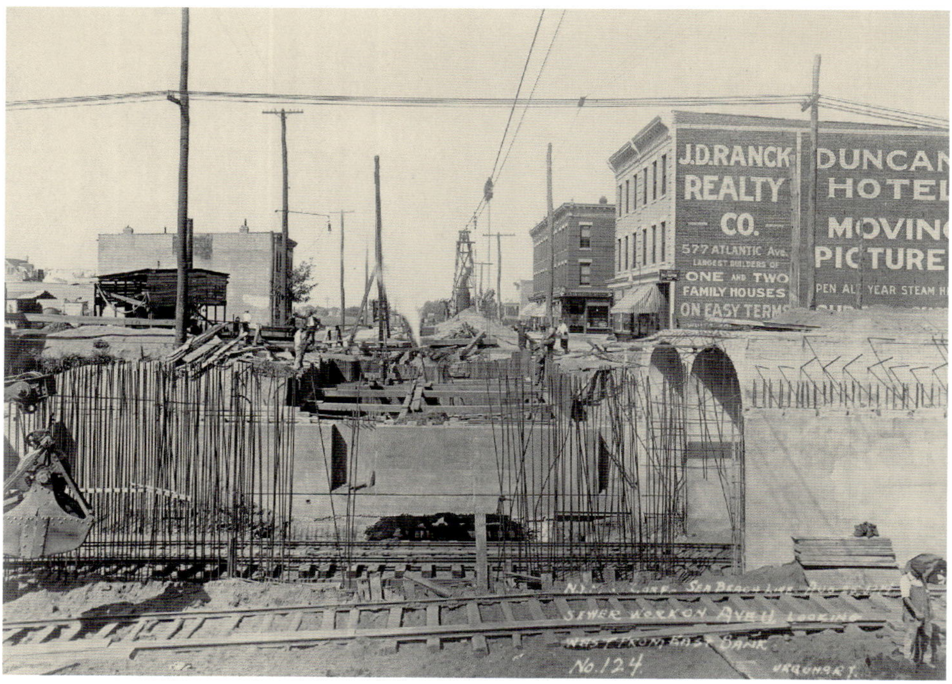

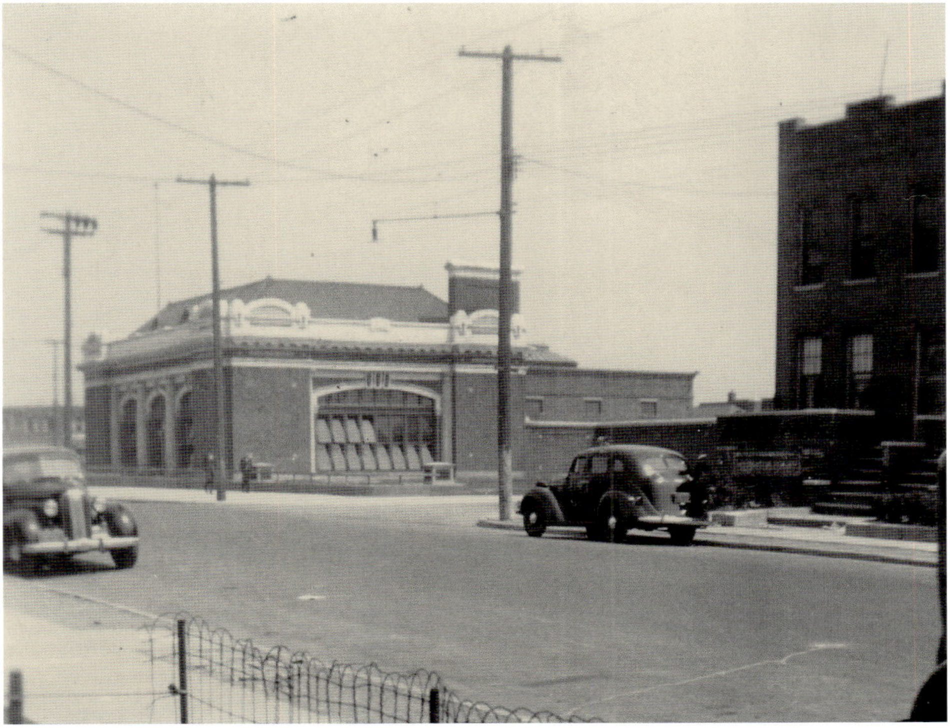

The sewers of western Gravesend converge inside this Beaux-Arts-style pumping station at 84 Avenue V, designed by architect Albert Martin around 1917. A storm water outlet connected to the station in the 1920s drained Hubbard's Creek (the main tributary of Coney Island Creek), which snaked southeast between Twenty-fifth Avenue and Shell Road. The dried marshland now holds the Coney Island Rail Yards (opened in 1926) and the Marlboro Projects (completed in 1958). The Avenue V Pumping Station is being refurbished after decades of neglect.

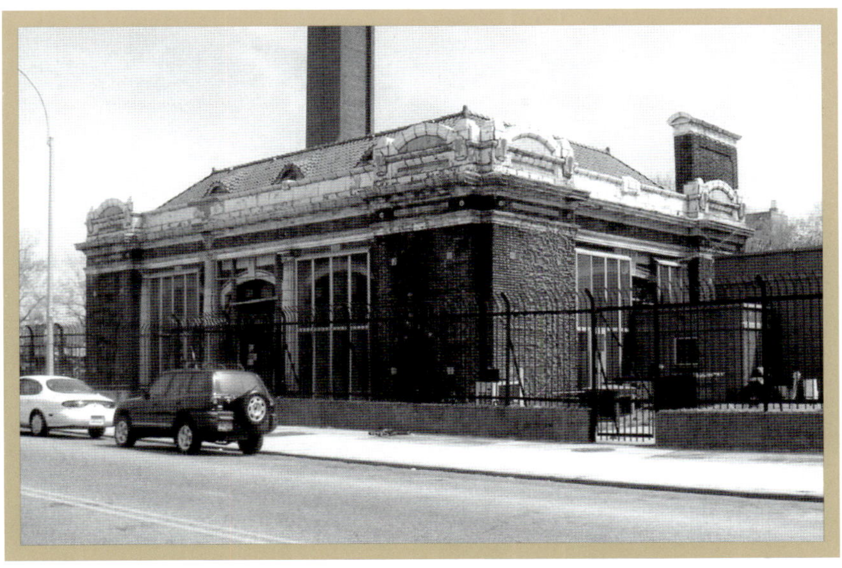

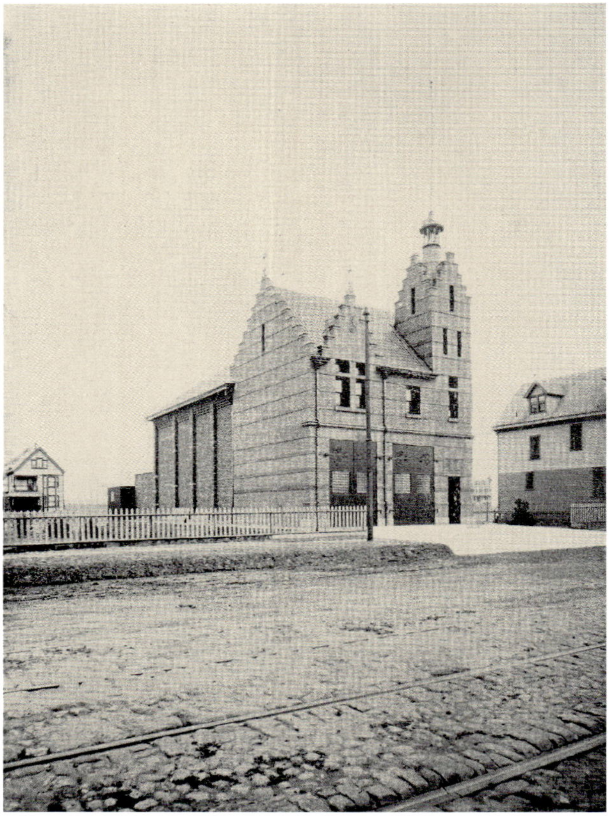

The late-19th-century suburban development of Bensonhurst-by-the-Sea straddled the border between the former Kings County towns of New Utrecht and Gravesend. To serve the community, the expanded City of Brooklyn built this handsome firehouse between 1895 and 1896 for Engine Company 53 (now Engine Company 253) at 2425–2427 Eighty-sixth Street. Except for its missing cupola and gable-top finials, the Dutch Renaissance Revival–style structure designed by Parfitt Brothers, architects, remains largely intact. It gained landmark status in 1998. (Courtesy of the New-York Historical Society.)

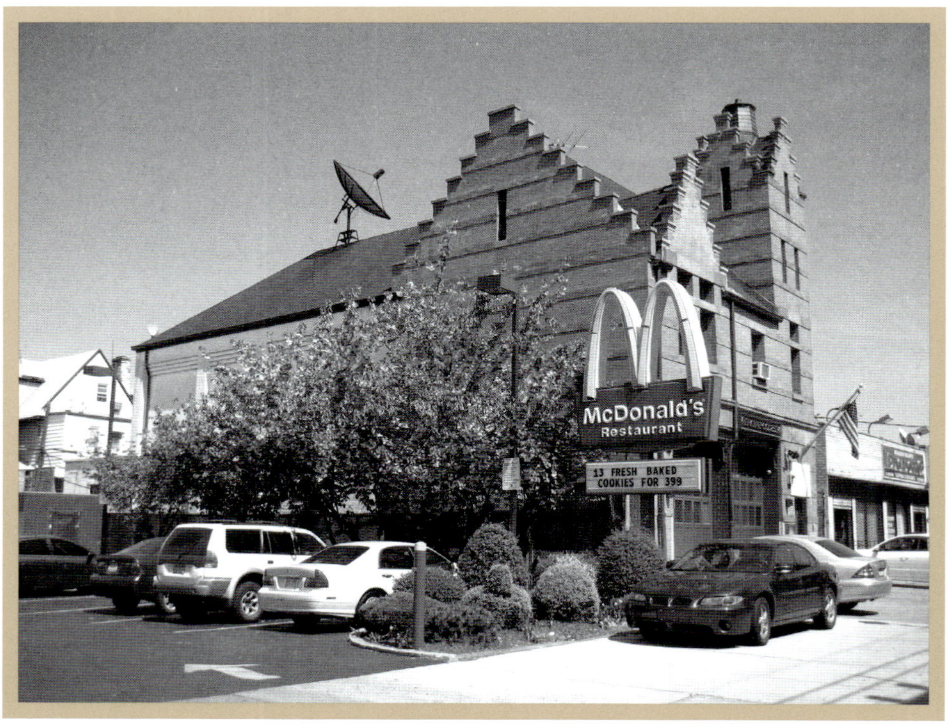

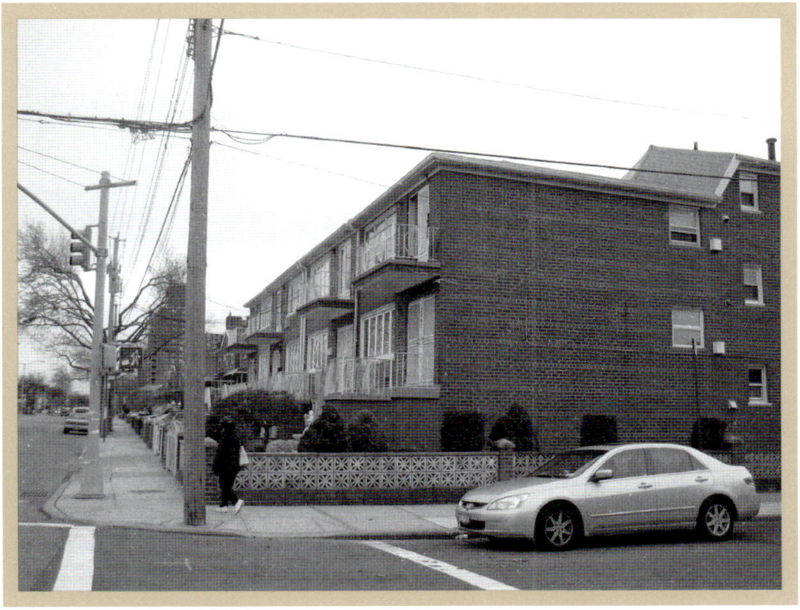

Ulmer Park opened in 1893 at the foot of Twenty-fifth Avenue in Gravesend Beach. Established by brewer William Ulmer (1833–1907), the grounds, billed as "The Only Family Resort on Long Island," soon came under the management of William Texter (1850–1930). His Ulmer Park Casino, seen here about 1908, opened in 1896 at 2502 Cropsey Avenue. Prohibition padlocked Texter's watering hole in 1925, and Ulmer Park was gone by 1940, when the Belt Parkway cut through the site.

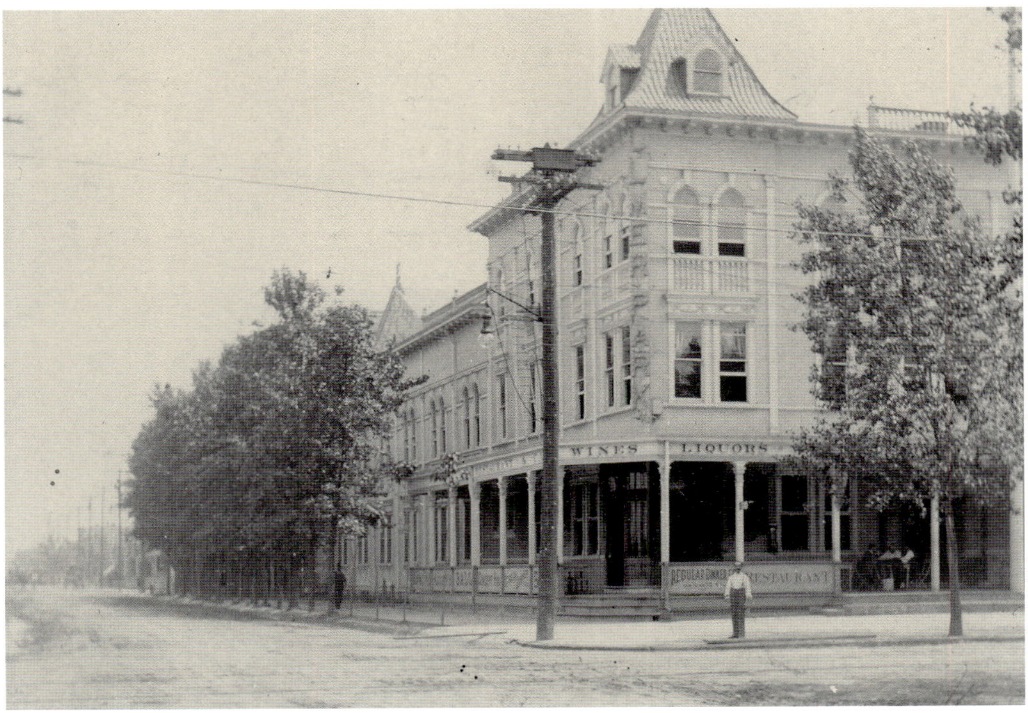

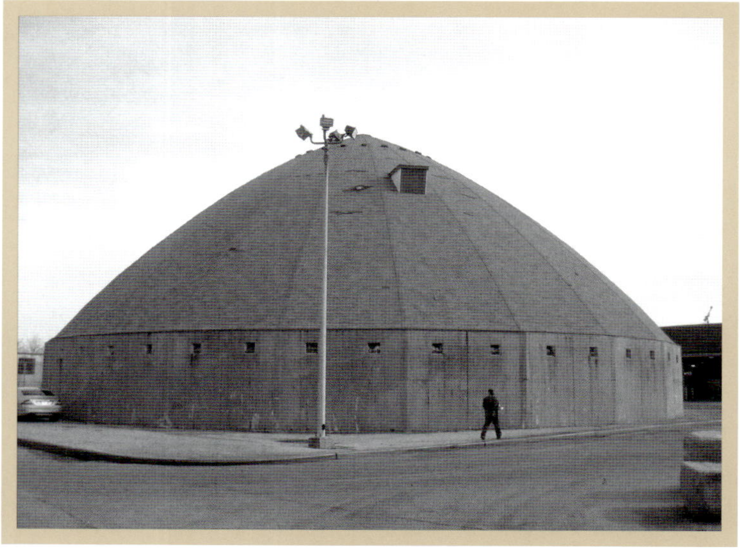

In 1904, a summertime colony called Camp City sprang up on the shore of Gravesend Bay between Twenty-fifth Avenue and Bay Forty-first Street, behind Ulmer Park. Like the buildings in other seasonal communities around New York (such as Rockaway Beach, Queens, and Gerritsen Beach, Brooklyn), Camp City's makeshift "tent-cottages" evolved into year-round residences. The Belt Parkway severed access to the site, which now holds two massive winter salt domes for the New York City Department of Sanitation.

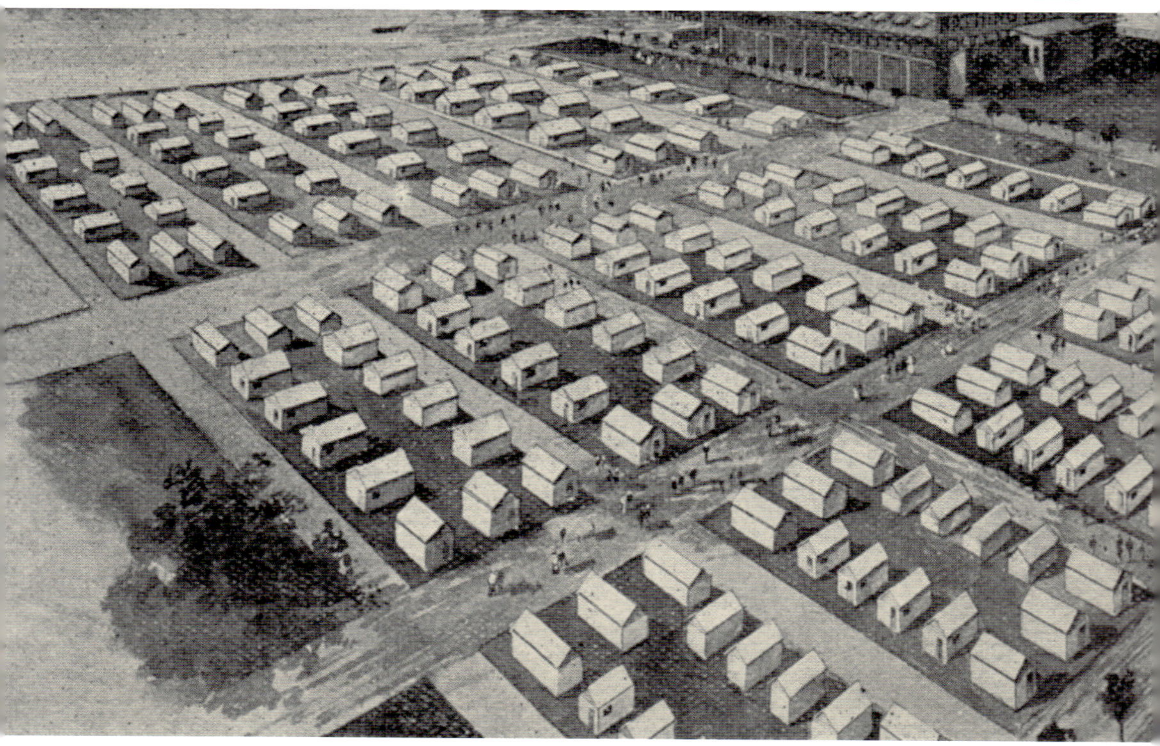

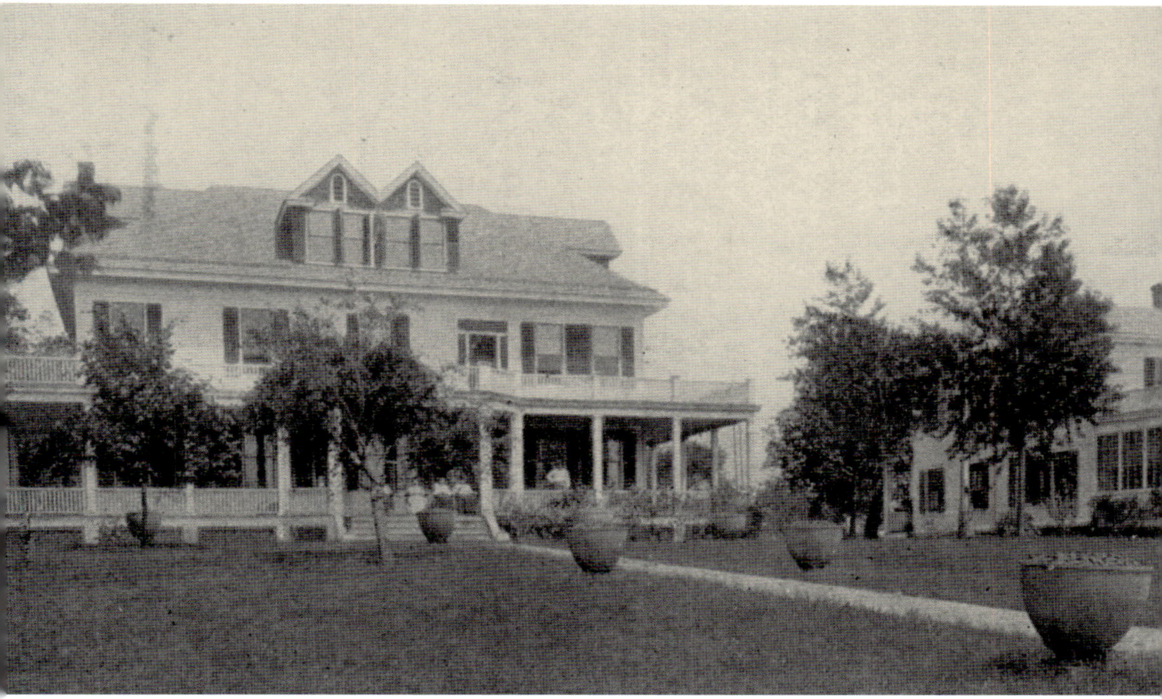

The German Home for Recreation of Women and Children opened in 1898 at the foot of Twenty-seventh Avenue. The Dreier and Offerman families donated land and funds for the home, where convalescent (and probably unwed) mothers and their children enjoyed restorative "quietness, good care," and the "bracing sea air" off Gravesend Bay. When it closed in 1933, the grounds became Dreier-Offerman Park, since partly renamed for Calvert Vaux, the architect and codesigner of Central Park, who drowned offshore in 1895.

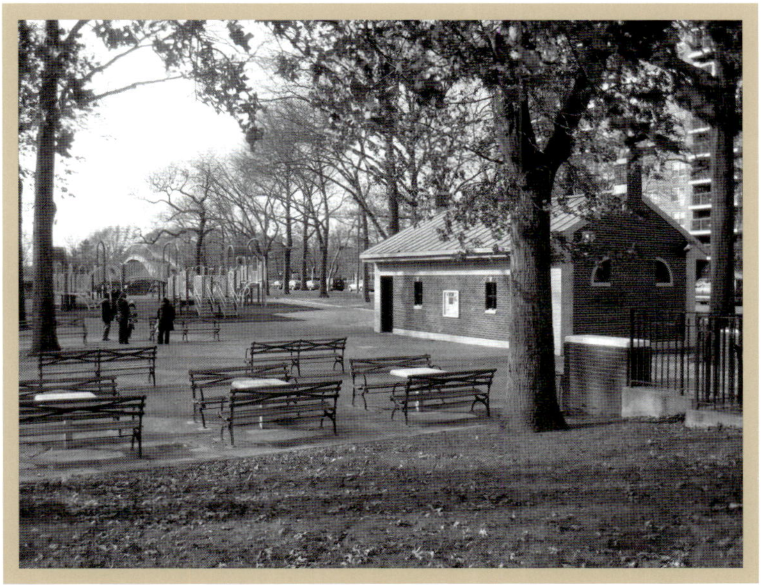

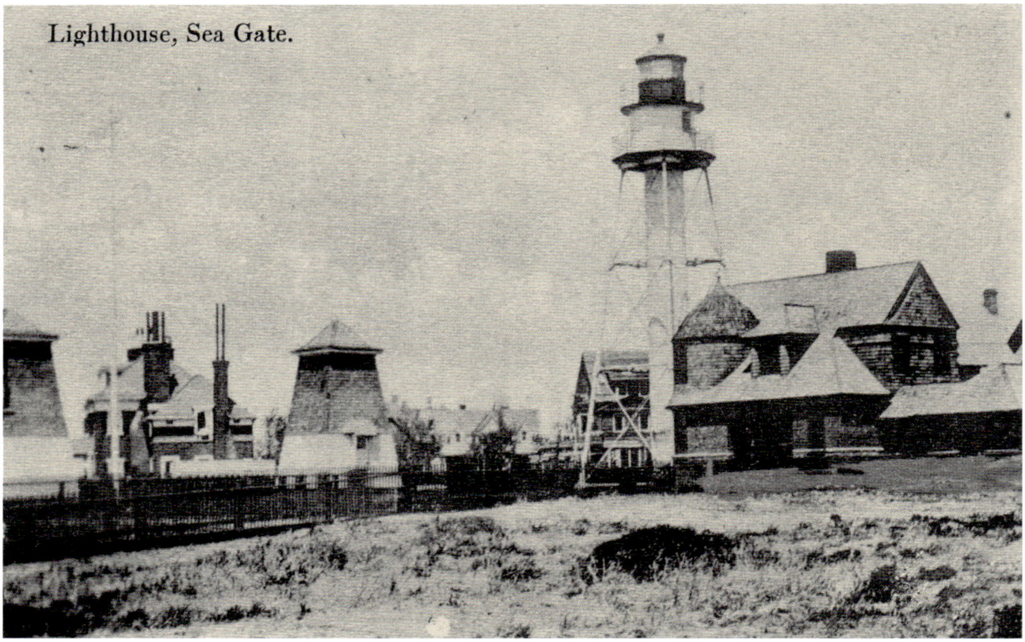

The Coney Island Light Station on the shore between Beach Forty-sixth and Forty-seventh Streets at Norton's Point, Sea Gate, went into operation in 1890. Currently lit by a 1,000-watt bulb, its red flash is visible 14 miles at sea. The light has had just six keepers. Its last, Frank Schubert (1915–2003), assumed his post in 1960 and manned it even after the mechanism was automated. At his death, Schubert was the last civilian lighthouse keeper in the United States.

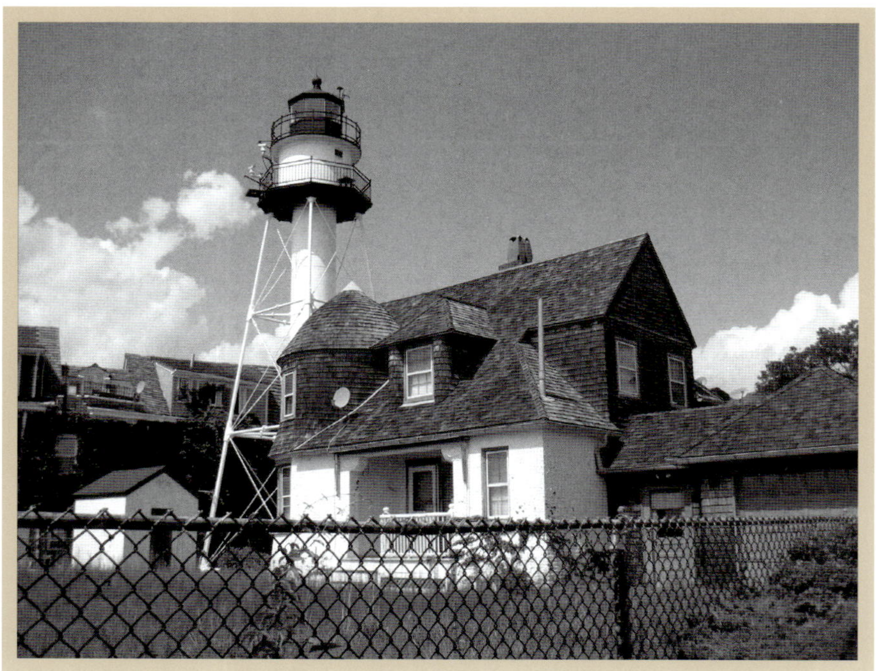

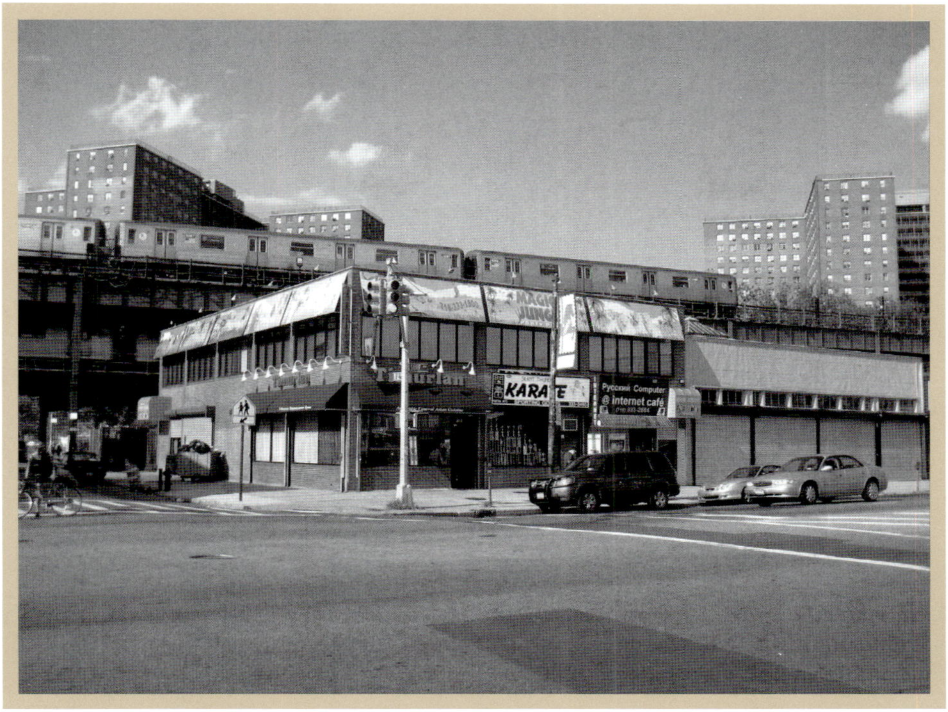

Elephantine Colossus, Coney Island's unlikely elephant-shaped hotel, stood facing the Atlantic Ocean on the north side of Surf Avenue just east of West Twelfth Street. Built in 1884 by J. Mason Kirby to the design of architect James V. Lafferty Jr., it never succeeded as a hotel and later held tobacco shops and a souvenir bazaar. The immediate neighborhood became one of Coney Island's seediest, where prostitution sold under the phrase "seeing the elephant." The tin-skinned wooden pachyderm burned spectacularly on September 27, 1896.

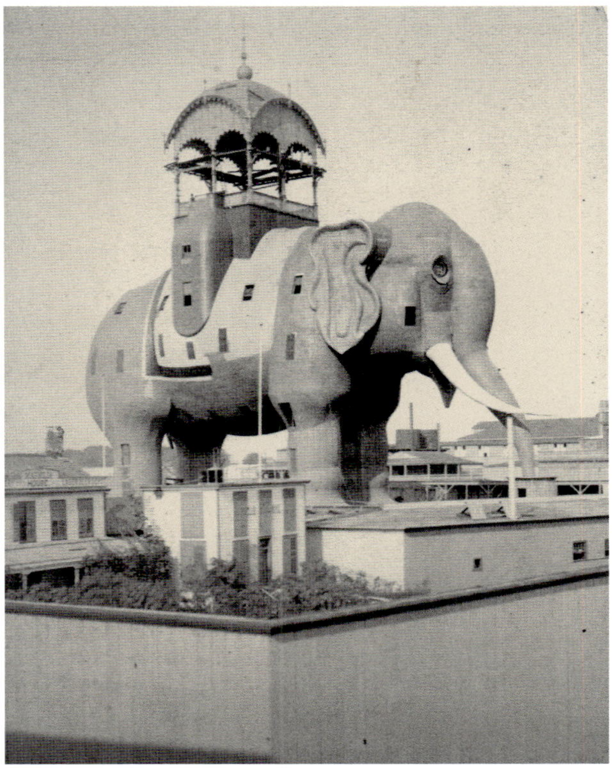